CW00481543

KD42138 ω31 6·p
+1

CHRISTIAN SCHMIDT-HÄUER

GORBACHEV

THE PATH TO POWER

**With an Appendix on the Soviet economy
by Maria Huber**

Translated by
Ewald Osers and Chris Romberg

Edited by
John Man

I.B.TAURIS & Co Ltd
Publishers
London

Published by I.B.Tauris & Co. Ltd.
3 Henrietta Street
Covent Garden
London WC2E 8PW
England

Copyright © 1986 R. Piper GmbH Munich

English translation copyright © 1986 I.B.Tauris & Co. Ltd.

All rights reserved. Except for brief quotations in a review, this book, or any part thereof, must not be reproduced in any form without permission in writing from the Publisher.

British Library Cataloguing in Publication Data

Schmidt-Häuer, Christian
  Gorbachev, The Path to Power.
  1. Gorbachev, Mikhail Sergeevich   2. Statesman –
  Soviet Union – Biography
  I. Title   II. Michael Gorbachow.   *English*
  947.085′4′0924 DK290.3.G67

  ISBN 1-85043-015-2

Printed in Great Britain by
Redwood Burn Ltd, Trowbridge, Wiltshire

ACKNOWLEDGEMENTS

This book would not have come into being without constant discussion with my colleague Mária Huber. I owe her my greatest thanks for numerous inspirations and many improvements. I also thank my Soviet friends and acquaintances who time and again guided me with courage and trust. I owe particular thanks to the brilliant analytical mind of Alexander Arnot, the German Embassy, with whom I shared many years in Moscow, and to Shirley and Raymond Benson of the American Embassy, whose understanding of Eastern European cultures has been invaluable.

Finally I owe special thanks to my sympathetic and patient editor, John Man, to my translators Ewald Osers and Chris Romberg, and to my publisher Iradj Bagherzade, whose advice and suggestions have decisively contributed to many passages in this book.

Christian Schmidt-Häuer
Hamburg, January 1986.

CONTENTS

Introduction

Shortly after Mikhail Gorbachev attained supreme authority as General Secretary of the Communist Party, he made a symbolic choice. He set February 25 as the date for the opening of the 27th Party Congress in 1986. February 25 has particular significance in Soviet history. It was the date on which Nikita Khrushchev concluded his disclosure of Stalin's crimes to the 20th Party Congress 30 years earlier.

Stalin's mass terror had at last been formally condemned. But of Khrushchev's revelations about "The Cult of Personality and its Consequences" — that was the title of the Secret Speech — only the words "Cult of Personality" were remembered. The economic and administrative "consequences" of Stalinism were quietly ignored, shamefacedly veiled, until now.

The social transformation Mikhail Gorbachev is seeking to achieve is the second attempt at de-Stalinization. Khrushchev had fought with Stalin's shadow spontaneously, individually and personally. Gorbachev, 30 years later, is trying to mount a well-planned, large-scale assault on Stalin's legacy — the Soviet Union's hide-bound, centralized economic system.

Khrushchev took the field against a terror which had

threatened the lives of all. Gorbachev leads a campaign against subtler forms of destruction: corruption, alcoholism, inefficiency. Khrushchev tried to eliminate Stalin's confederates — Molotov, Kaganovich, Voroshilov, Malenkov — and force legality on the bureaucracy. Gorbachev aims to replace a whole generation and force that same bureaucracy to change by insisting on results.

Despite all his power, Khrushchev remained a villager. His communism had a vigour, despite the absurdity of his prophecies. He appealed to the proletariat as a populist. Gorbachev, too, is a populist. But he is more deliberate and more prudent; cooler, if no less bold; more predictable, if no less calculating. Where Khrushchev liked to show off as the bucolic peasant, aping the founders of communism with empty demands for world revolution, Gorbachev wishes to appear as a concerned statesman, appealing for global partnership, pointing to Lenin, the later Lenin, Lenin the *real* politician, to legitimize his programme of reform.

The course Gorbachev has chosen has amazed and fascinated observers. But it was not entirely unforeseen.

From the mid-1970's onwards, the Soviet elite showed a yearning for change. At that time, which I spent as a correspondent in Moscow, an unexpected gulf gradually opened up before my eyes. On one hand, at official receptions and in daily television news bulletins, I saw a superannuated Party leadership, clinging to an unreal view of the world, compensating for their dwindling competence by presenting each other with medals. On the other hand, in day-to-day life, in enterprises, institutes and libraries, I met the representatives of a younger elite, who viewed the world curiously and neutrally, undogmatically and with a readiness to learn.

These young people were not dissidents. They neither idolized the West nor condemned socialism. They belonged to no particular camp. They were not true believers in communism, but nor did they hate it. They had faith in their own strengths, and wanted to use those strengths to upgrade the quality of their lives and achieve a better, more rationally organized society. Though they did not expect such changes from the Old Guard — the bureaucrats and administrators who had grown senile under Brezhnev — and scarcely considered the possibility of a new leadership, their lack of cynicism convinced me that the Soviet Union contained a wealth of reserves waiting to be utilized for the creation of a more humane world.

It was Andropov who first began to tap those reserves. With the majority of the population yearning vaguely for a "strong man," Andropov, then KGB Director, opened two campaigns, firstly against corruption (though the onslaught was more a means of seizing power than an end in itself) and then for a more effective social system. It was Andropov, himself ailing, who presented the man who would, he believed, bear the hopes of the newly emerging younger generation — Mikhail Gorbachev, a newcomer from the northern Caucasus, who had become Central Committee Secretary in 1978 at the age of only 47, and had entered the Politburo as a full member before his 50th birthday.

The change-over was without precedent in the history of the Soviet Union. This book describes how it occurred and examines the opportunity it offers for the future development of the Soviet Union and its relations with the outside world, particularly with the United States and Europe.

Have peace and reason a new chance under Gorbachev? Can the desire for peace overcome the dead weight of armaments programmes and the influence of Soviet and American defence industries? If the human contact established by Gorbachev and Reagan at Geneva is anything to go by, if the warmth of their New Year greetings means anything, if the spate of disarmament proposals flowing between Moscow and Washington in the first months of 1986 have any substance, then the answer is a qualified yes.

But Gorbachev's peace offensive is not an expression of pure idealism. It is the international consequence of the need for domestic reform. Gorbachev must secure peace abroad if his country is to advance at home. There are dangers on both sides. Gorbachev's reforms may falter (as Khrushchev's did — one lesson to be learned from Russian history is that it is very hard for any one leader to impose his will on such a huge and inert society). In that case, the rationale behind his peace offensive would collapse. Or the Atlantic Alliance, its members' interests diverging on the issue of Reagan's Strategic Defence Initiative (SDI, or "Star Wars"), may turn against Gorbachev's tactics, forcing him to re-arm and threatening his reform programme. Never before have the two issues — the development of the Soviet economy and world security — been so intimately connected. Now, as never before, the West must bear its share of responsibility for both.

1

"A Red Star Rises": An Overview

London, Saturday, December 15, 1984: Mikhail Gorbachev, as yet unknown to the public in the West, arrived at the head of a Soviet parliamentary delegation who were on a routine exchange visit as guests of the House of Commons. Gorbachev was officially no more than a Politburo Member, Central Committee Secretary and Chairman of the Foreign Affairs Commission of the Supreme Soviet; but there was a feeling that the visit could have a significance way beyond its official purpose. Besides being the youngest Politburo Member, he was heir-apparent to the aging, ailing Konstantin Chernenko. This was the first visit by a high-ranking Soviet leader since Premier Alexei Kosygin came to London in 1967. His every word and gesture would be watched for some insight into the younger generation of future leaders. Would he be merely another grim bureaucrat, a younger version of the old men who had ruled the Soviet Union for the previous two decades? Or might his rise mark a genuine break with the past?

Even on arrival that December noon, he seemed indeed to be something different, dapperly dressed in grey pinstripe suit and trilby hat, as easy and relaxed as any West European parliamentarian, not at all the remote apparatchik.

Nor, apparently, was this mere window-dressing. That afternoon, he visited the British Museum, where he was subjected to a little incident that might have been designed to test his responses. A group of some 40 demonstrators chanted: "Gorbachev, where is Sakharov?" a reference to the dissident scientist banished for his activities. The visit got off to a good start, with a look at a first edition of the *Communist Manifesto*, a second edition of *Das Kapital*, and the desk where Karl Marx actually worked on the book. "If people don't like Marxism," joked Gorbachev, "they should blame the British Museum." Then on he went, moving across the wood-panelled reading room with a scholar's intensity, past the Chinese exhibits, to view the ancient Egyptian room. There, in among the labyrinth of showcases two emigres suddenly appeared at his side shouting, "Freedom for the Ukraine!" at the tops of their voices. For a few horrified seconds, there was confusion as half a dozen policemen ejected the demonstrators, still yelling. The British security officer put on an embarrassed smile, and the small caravan of Soviet visitors trooped on.

There are several ways Gorbachev could have seen the incident — as a put-up job, officially sanctioned by the British; as an indication of freedoms unknown in the Soviet Union; as a symbol of the West's anti-Soviet hostility; or merely as the result of a negligible error in security. Whatever Gorbachev may have thought about the incident, he didn't show it. Then, and later, as a British official said, "A smile was never far from his face."

But the next few days revealed that there was more to him than discretion and charm. He had a stature, the aura of a statesman. In part, this impression derived from the way he looked and acted — the features firm, but not coarse (and unaffected by the red birthmark on his powerful, balding cranium); the mouth suggesting a combination of sensuality and determination; the expression — in particular, the lines at the corners of his eyes — hinting at the presence of humour and shrewdness; the gaze direct and intelligent; the solid build of a peasant without a trace of clumsiness. Intense, but not tense. No actor's tricks —

none of the theatrical gestures in which Brezhnev indulged, nothing like Gromyko's habit of alternating a poker face with rolling eyes. Gorbachev would not display petulance in public, as Gromyko did in April 1977 by snapping pencils when listening to President Carter's proposals on disarmament.

Above all, Gorbachev was constantly attentive. In conversation, he posed question after question — asking after career, earnings, attitudes — questions that showed off both his education and his preparedness. He was fond of pointed sallies — "Do you yourself believe what you are telling me?" was one of his favourites — but he never resorted to cliche. It was as if he were playing a brisk game of verbal chess, constantly on the offensive.

He lost no opportunities for displaying his qualities. On his visit to Britain, he was at ease with everyone he met, including churchmen and Conservatives. When, in Westminster Abbey, he came to the tomb of Charles Darwin, he asked the Dean about the compatibility of Christian teaching with Darwinism. When the former Conservative minister Norman St. John Stevas questioned him about violations of religious freedom and human rights in the Soviet Union, Gorbachev countered not as his predecessors would have done with a ponderous and precise lecture in praise of the Soviet way of life, but with a quick thrust of his own: "I could quote a few facts about human rights in the United Kingdom. You persecute entire communities, entire nationalities," — an allusion to Northern Ireland — "You have 2.3 million unemployed. You govern *your* society. And we'll govern *ours*." Short and to the point (and even unintentionally generous: Britain had more than 3.2 million unemployed at the time).

Heads of firms praised his well-briefed expertise. Government and Opposition leaders were equally impressed by his manners and conversation. The journalists were flattered by his courteous attentiveness. Although, as usual, all requests for interviews were refused, the refusals had a certain elegance: "Mr. Gorbachev would like to thank you for your interest and your request for an interview. Unfortunately, he is not at this moment able to comply with your request." At a luncheon given for him by Sir Geoffrey Howe in the candle-lit Tudor splendour of Hampton Court, Gorbachev, as if performing in some TV commercial, delayed his toast by making a passing reference to the delicious coffee before softly yet firmly stating the real political purpose behind his trip. Unless militarization of space was prevented, Gorbachev said, "it is unrealistic to hope for an end to the nuclear arms race." Yet in the next breath he tactfully recalled the joint sacrifices of the Second World War, with a specific mention of the bombing of Coventry.

The British press hailed him as a "golden boy." The *Sunday Times* praised him to the skies: "A red star rises in the East," read one headline. In a BBC discussion, two Members of Parliament, apparently seeing him as a sort of democrat manqué, referred to him as their colleague, as if he were a fellow parliamentarian. Denis Healey, Labour's Shadow Foreign Secretary, waxed positively poetic: "Emotions flicker over a face of unusual sensitivity," he said, "like summer breezes on a pond." The Tories — delighted to be wooed by the Kremlin ahead of all other Europeans — were equally impressed. Even Mrs. Thatcher, not normally given to expressions of warmth, enthused about her guest. "I like him. We can do business together," she pronounced.

Certainly, Moscow's engaging negotiator did considerable business. The performance in London was a dress rehearsal both for his own later appearances in the world, and also for a concerted attack on President Reagan's space proposals, the Strategic Defence Initiative (SDI or "Star Wars"). Moscow chose London for its launch because Mrs. Thatcher, with her special influence on Ronald Reagan, seemed to the Kremlin leaders to be the best person to explain Western Europe's misgivings about the American project to the White House. Gorbachev made his point well. Mrs. Thatcher was said to believe that the Soviets were just as anxious as Britain to prevent an extension of the arms race in space. In consequence, when Gorbachev came to power in Moscow two months later, he was in a stronger position to bring Soviet influence to bear on the Star Wars issue, and exploit the tension between the USA and her Western European allies.

But the British visit had another effect. Gorbachev showed he could challenge the American President with Reagan's own weapons — showmanship. None of Gorbachev's predecessors had ever chosen such a course before. Wooing the media, courting publicity in the style of a Western electioneer, displaying charm, promoting the image of the family man, allowing the media to catch glimpses of his private life — these were novelties for a Soviet leader, ones that were to be further exploited during his trip to Paris in October 1985 and at the Geneva summit in November.

Thus, when Gorbachev came to power in March, he had by his skilful performances in London already supplied the Western film and photo archives with the kind of material they needed to welcome him onto the world stage. Here at long last was a man who was willing and able to behave in a way the West understood. Ever since Khrushchev's death, television stations had had the thankless task of trying to produce exciting footage from increasingly dreary Party bureaucrats — Brezhnev, whose whole stock-in-trade seemed to consist of back-slapping bonhomie; the retiring Andropov, who had his propagandists in the West whisper only about his indisputable intelligence and reassuringly intellectual interest in literature; and Chernenko, who was never more than a grey shadow on the television screens.

Gorbachev, by contrast, radiated a double splendour, his own and that of his wife, Raisa. From the moment she stepped out of the aircraft at Heathrow dressed in a black, fur-trimmed cossack coat, her hair tinted reddish-brown, her hosts and the British press enthused about her extravagantly. Whether she spoke in catch-phrases (at one point she startled her hosts by saying, "See you later, alligator") or discussed culture or haute-couture, Raisa Gorbacheva captivated those around her. She was not shy about expressing her opinions and requests, but with her engaging smile, intelligence and natural charm, the popular press loved her. It gossiped about her clothes, her shopping habits, even her earrings. "This woman not only costs me a lot of nerves but also a lot of money," her husband was reported to have joked, displaying the safe, familiar humour of any Western politician out campaigning.

Along with fashion-conscious, worldly self-confidence, the Gorbachevs also cultivated the folksy image of an ordinary family living an ordinary family life. As if for all the world forgetting he was heir-apparent to supreme power in the Soviet Union, Gorbachev kept showing photos of his seven-year-old granddaughter, Oksana. "She complains that she never sees me — except on Sundays, and then only for a couple of hours," he said. "I work every day from half past seven in the morning till half past nine in the evening." Every new detail was solemnly noted by a press corps unaccustomed to such trivia from Soviet leaders.

There could be no doubt that as a campaign to win over the western media, Gorbachev's British visit was a triumph.

For insiders, though, Gorbachev's performance did not come as a complete surprise.

In June 1984 he had, as a deliberate political gesture, attended the funeral of the Chairman of the Italian Communist Party, Enrico Berlinguer, the "father" of Euro-communism. Gorbachev's reputed patron, Moscow's long-term guardian of the ideological grail, Mikhail Suslov, had always bitterly and dogmatically condemned Berlinguer right up until his death in January 1982. Yet Gorbachev, at the burial of this champion of reform, proclaimed: "Berlinguer's criticism was not in vain." Much to their surprise, he gave a dinner for the leading Italian comrades at the Soviet Embassy. Whatever Gorbachev really thought of Euro-communism or its Italian variant, he made this an opportunity to reduce tension between the two parties, turning it to good personal effect.

And before that, in May 1983, when he visited Canada, he had put on a show of another kind. He began by talking mainly as an expert in agriculture, acting the role of farmer. On a cattle ranch in Alberta, he posed in a cowboy hat and ate at a barbecue. He also donned a peaked cap with "Heinz" on it, and allowed himself to be photographed with the ketchup manufacturer. According to *Newsweek*, he looked like an American presidential candidate among his supporters in New Hampshire.

But back in Ottawa, submitting to questions by Canadian parliamentarians, he changed roles, showing himself as a hard-hitting politician. During the ninety-minute discussion, which ranged over Soviet nuclear rearmament, the occupation of Afghanistan and human rights, he accused Allan Lawrence, the former Conservative member of the Cabinet, of being "a victim of the spy mania spread by America." Allan McKinnon, a Member of the Canadian Parliament and defence expert, crossed swords with Gorbachev on the subject of SS-20 missiles and concluded: "He'd make an excellent politician. He talks as if he was in the middle of an election campaign."

On February 24 1985, two weeks before Konstantin Chernenko's death, Gorbachev moved his campaign to Soviet soil. On that sunny winter's day he appeared in the ancient, palatial House of Soviet Architects to cast his vote in the politically unimportant regional elections. Western journalists had received advance notice of his arrival.

For the occasion, Gorbachev brought along with him not only his wife Raisa and his daughter Irina but also his granddaughter Oksana. The little girl was allowed to drop her grandfather's ballot-paper into the ballot-box. The delighted photographers wanted to have the scene repeated. "Even I have only one vote," remarked Gorbachev with a smile, again the kind of quip that was bound to go down well with the media.

Soviet viewers, meanwhile, were seeing on their screens a macabre demonstration staged by Brezhnev's Old Guard in a last desperate attempt to hold on to the power that was slipping through their fingers. Konstantin Chernenko, now terminally ill, was shown casting his vote in a sick-room decorated to look like a polling station. The old Party chief, scarcely capable of movement or speech, was accompanied and fussed over by Viktor Grishin, the Chairman of the Moscow Party Committee. The sole purpose of this gruesome scene was to present Grishin as Chernenko's favoured heir to the post of General Secretary.

A fortnight later, however, on the evening of March 10 1985, a few hours after Chernenko's death, it was clear that the power of the veterans was broken. True, at that late-night meeting of the Politburo Gorbachev's long-standing rival Grigori Romanov proposed Viktor Grishin for the post of General Secretary. But the vigorous pleas of Foreign Minister Gromyko and KGB chief Chebrikov in favour of Gorbachev finally ensured the take-over by a representative of the younger generation.

Nine days after his 54th birthday, on March 11, Gorbachev was elected by the Plenum of the Central Committee to be General Secretary of the Party and thus the eighth leader of the Soviet Union.

A new style of leader had emerged.

It now became clear that his style was not merely good PR. It reflected real authority within the power structure. The speed of his accession showed that.

Ever since the early 1960's, the Soviet Union had become increasingly fossilized. Change was vital, the more so as death began to claim the Kremlin leaders one by one. Within a mere 28 months, the Party and state heads Leonid Brezhnev, Yuri Andropov and Konstantin Chernenko, along with Dmitri Ustinov, one of the most influential Members of the Politburo after the General Secretary, had all been laid to rest under the Kremlin Wall.

And now, in Gorbachev, the Soviet Union had suddenly produced a man who acted as if he were St. George, promising to slay dragons — America's Star Wars, the Soviet planning bureaucracy — and to lead his empire out of economic calamity and technological backwardness into a new age. "Only an intensive, highly-developed economy," Gorbachev said, addressing ideological officials in Moscow on December 10 1984, "can guarantee a consolidation of our country's position in the international arena and permit it to enter the next millennium as a great, flourishing state."

What chance of success has he? Is Gorbachev's showmanship mere gloss, or an indication that radical change is imminent?

We shall see in the next chapter that in the context of Russian history it is hard for any individual, however powerful, to have lasting impact. Nevertheless, Gorbachev's rise clearly foreshadows significant changes within the Soviet Union. For one thing, the way in which he came to power was unprecedented, and had startling implications.

Until November 1978 Mikhail Gorbachev was nothing more than a local politician — Party Secretary of the Stavropol Region in the Caucasus. A mere six and a half years later, he became General Secretary, despite being by far the youngest Member of the Politburo by whom he was elected, indeed the youngest Party chief in all Eastern Europe.

His youth was not the only thing that was surprising about his rise. He had also been involved in Soviet agriculture, an activity fatal for the careers of many before him. Agricultural experts in the Party leadership have all been broken by agricultural calamity: Dmitri Polyansky, Politburo Member and Minister of Agriculture, was pushed off to Japan as ambassador in 1976; Fedor Kulakov, Politburo Member and Central Committee Secretary, who committed suicide in 1978, aged only 60, was rumoured to have been involved in violent clashes about agricultural policy immediately prior to his death. Yet Gorbachev, Kulakov's successor, became Central Committee Secretary responsible for the agricultural sector in 1978, and continued on his road unharmed.

Thus, as Chernenko trembled on the verge of death, for the first time since the Revolution there was none of the traditional uncertainty about the transfer of power. When the time came, the change was smooth.

There is an important implication in that smooth transfer of power that belies the Western cliches about unyielding dogmatists cut off behind impregnable Kremlin walls. Soviet leaders who identify and prepare a successor over a lengthy period, even though his responsibility for agriculture might have weighed heavily against him, even though his younger rivals might find their own progress blocked for perhaps a couple of decades, and who then tolerate criticism of the Old Guard by that successor, are not totally shackled by dogma.

But such flexibility is relative. It does not make Gorbachev a "liberal" or a man whom naive Western politicians may expect to be a supporter of human rights. A man who was hoisted into the saddle by Andropov, the former Secret Police chief, a man who still bases himself on Andropov's guard and on KGB confidants, does not dream of some sort of Soviet Camelot.

He is in some ways the product of the Old Guard. The supreme custodian of ideological purity, Mikhail Suslov, who died in 1982 and who from 1939 to 1944 had been First Party Secretary of the Stavropol Regional Committee, had for a time been one of his protectors. Fedor Kulakov, who in the late 1960's made a similar meteoric rise to the Central Committee and subsequently to the Politburo, also accelerated Gorbachev's career. Kulakov, a moderate supporter of cautious reforms, closely co-operated with the rising Gorbachev as Party chief of the Stavropol Regional Committee between 1960 and 1964. The third man, Gorbachev's most important supporter, was Yuri Andropov. As Party chief Andropov groomed his young "fellow countryman" — they were both from the Stavropol Region — as a candidate for his succession.

Nevertheless, Gorbachev is much more than an Old Guard product, for three main reasons: his age, his origins — both of which in part determine his unusual mix of dynamism and solidity — and the state of the nation.

Gorbachev was born in 1931, during the famine which resulted from Stalin's brutal enforcement of his central planning system. Aged ten at the time of the German invasion and still a student at Stalin's death, he was the first Politburo Member whose age precluded him from playing a role as a frontline soldier. Accordingly, in his speeches he sees the "Great Patriotic War" in less heroic, more realistic terms.

Gorbachev and his generation, who were not even indirectly involved in Stalin's terror, have no feelings of guilt about that period. They have no need therefore to compensate by constantly harping on the epic nature of the fight against Hitler, as the Old Guard did. The creation of the central planning system, which began with Stalin's appalling human sacrifices on the altar of industrialization and which was defended by the generation after Stalin, is to these younger men just so much ancient history, history in which they had no part and which they do not have to justify.

Here lies the real divide between the generations. It was this absence of any historical baggage that helped smooth Gorbachev's road to power, even while the Old Guard was still in control. A less blinkered and prejudiced generation was free to challenge established dogma. Matters previously taboo increasingly became subjects for public discussion.

It was the economy that progressively became the dominant factor, even in foreign policy. For the old guardians of communist dogma, such as Mikhail Suslov, it would have been tantamount to treason to admit, even indirectly, that the collectivization of agriculture had been a disaster. To the younger Soviet elite, however, the land is no longer an issue of ideology but of practicality, of balancing economic efficiency with centralized political power.

Being less rooted in tradition, his attitude towards industry was also very different from that of his older colleagues. The old bureaucrats could see Soviet world power only in terms of overwhelming heavy industry. Machine tools, aircraft, ships and missiles were the emblems of progress. Consumer goods were troublesome concessions to the masses. Gorbachev, on the other hand, would like (with admittedly very limited means) to realize a policy proclaimed a quarter of a century ago by the Soviet economist Yevgeni Liberman: to combine increased consumption and increased production, to promote light industry as an incentive to economic efficiency, to lift the Soviet population out of its technological backwardness into the age of the microprocessor.

His influence he owes in part to his provincial origins in the Caucasus. He studied law in Moscow, but he maintained his ties with his native rural region, where he obtained a second degree in agronomy. His influence locally was one source of his later strength. Throughout Russian history some of the finest patriots have been men from the provinces, men who kept their ties with their native regions and at the same time stirred them out of their lethargy. This regional link enabled Gorbachev, immediately upon Andropov's assumption of power, to become his most important frontline man. It gave him a base from which to launch experiments.

Another element in his success is the progress of other countries, both Communist and non-Communist. The increasingly matter-of-fact way in which socialist countries, from China to East Germany, are now transforming their economies had undoubtedly lowered the thresholds of ideological inhibition in the Soviet Union. The fear of being left behind, isolated by dogma, became too great to resist. President Reagan's space initiative has heightened the ingrained anxiety over technological backwardness almost to the point of panic. This double pressure from the East and the West has given rise to fear for the future existence of the Soviet empire. Many a Soviet official must have secret worries along the lines of a judgement made by Samuel Huntington, the Harvard expert on international politics, who stated that in 50 years' time the USA would still be a great power, but questioned whether the Soviet Union would be.

Such gloomy prophecies no longer originate only in the West; they are now also supported by Soviet data (as Mária Huber makes clear in Appendix 1). The statistics show that industrial development during the final years of the Brezhnev era declined both in quantity and quality. In one vital industry — electronics — the decline has been greater than in the Soviet economy overall.

The top officials of the younger generation clearly understand that it is a country's ability to mass-produce high-technology goods that will decide whether that country can keep pace with the computer age. Gorbachev's men have already been able to force through both personnel and structural changes against the opposition of the central planning bureaucracy and the ministries. But neither knowledge nor power are in themselves enough to guarantee progress, for they are confronted by an economy that is spiralling downwards.

In the drive to develop high-technology goods, light industry must take the lead to ensure that the public is involved in the process. But in the Soviet Union, so far, the most capable specialists and the most modern computers have all gone to the armaments industry. Light industry and agriculture have atrophied, the latter no longer showing any growth at all. Production of consumer goods has dropped. The civilian population has little technological experience and shows little inventiveness. Fewer and fewer genuinely highly qualified specialists emerge from the educational process, which means that proportionately more of them are drafted into the armed forces, even fewer free for work in civilian life.

Although Gorbachev's university-trained advisers are aware of this vicious circle, their scope of action is very limited. If they are to modernize light industry and increase per-capita consumption by just one percent annually until 1990, gross investment and defence expenditure must increase by not more than 2.1 percent. The conflict between military interests and Gorbachev's hopes for a structural modernization of the Soviet economy may well be insoluble.

In greater detail, organizational shortcomings and technological backwardness — an inexhaustible source of colourful Western reports — were, for a while, more or less offset by the extensive employment of capital, raw materials and labour in the central industrial regions.

But this economic model no longer works, for three main reasons:

— resources in the western parts of the Soviet Union are yielding less and less. For the first time since the Second World War, oil production showed a decline in 1984 and 1985. Consequently,

— the processing industry can now expect investment on only a limited scale as more and more capital has to be used for the extraction of raw materials in increasingly inaccessible parts of Siberia;

— the birth rate in the most heavily industrialized western parts of the country has been declining for years. Abel Aganbegyan, the Director of the Novosibirsk Economic Institute, a man who clearly enjoys Gorbachev's particular respect, pointed out in the trade union daily *Trud* in 1984 that the supply of new manpower in this gigantic country has shrunk in the current Five-Year Plan to a mere three million, of whom 2.5 million come from Central Asia. This problem is aggravated by the poor health of young male workers, especially in the western regions. The life expectancy of men in the Soviet Union — largely due to excessive alcohol consumption — has dropped from 67 in 1964 to 62 in 1980; no other industrial society shows such a trend.

Gorbachev, in consequence, faces a gigantic task. When he came to power, he demonstrated right from the start, at Konstantin Chernenko's deathbed, that he was a man in a hurry.

As Chairman of the State Funeral Commission, he decreed the briefest mourning period and the shortest funeral ceremony for a Soviet leader since the October Revolution — an hour less than the rites for Brezhnev and Andropov — a seemingly trivial detail, but full of meaning in a Soviet context.

Chernenko's death was announced by the Soviet radio on Monday, March 11 1985, at 13.57 hours Moscow time — nearly 19 hours after the officially reported time of his death, 19.20 hours on March 10. Immediately after the announcement of his death came the news, almost like a deliberate gesture, that the new round of Geneva talks on nuclear arms limitation would begin, as planned, on the following day, March 12. A mere four hours after the news of Chernenko's death, Radio Moscow interrupted the solemn music to announce Gorbachev's election. The decisions in favour of Andropov (in November 1982) and Chernenko (in February 1984) had not been announced until several days after their respective predecessors' deaths. The prompt election of the new General Secretary was followed by a unique occurrence: although all daily newspapers carried the news of Chernenko's death on their front pages, there were no black borders and no photographs of the dead man. Instead, the front pages carried a photograph of his successor. Chernenko's photograph and the black border were relegated to page two.

The next day, Wednesday, March 13, was the day of the burial. But Gorbachev transformed the event from a ceremony commemorating the Old Guard into a demonstration on behalf of the new. A little more than a year previously, on February 14 1984, Chernenko — suffering from breathing difficulties, fluffing his lines and occasionally incomprehensible — had given the funeral oration for Andropov from the platform of the Lenin Mausoleum. Foreign Minister Gromyko and Defence Minister Ustinov did not allow Chernenko to be the sole speaker: both gave additional orations, as if to emphasise the limits of Chernenko's power. Gorbachev, by contrast, was flanked by no other high-ranking speakers (Politburo Member Grishin spoke in his capacity as Moscow's Party chief and special friend of Chernenko's, but following his defeat in the Politburo two days previously he was already finished politically). Gorbachev's vigorous voice rang out across Red Square, deliberately, if obliquely, declaring war on abuses which Chernenko had allowed: "We shall fight against all manifestations of humbug and slogan-mongering, arrogance and irresponsibility, against anything that runs counter to the norms of socialist life."

Even Chernenko's final journey — from the Lenin Mausoleum to the Kremlin Wall — was organized by the new leadership in a manner emphasising that it was eager to break with the past. The open coffin, draped in red and black, was carried only by Army officers, not, as had been the custom, also by Members of the Politburo. The final picture of the Old Guard leader seen by Soviet viewers was of his widow Anna bending over the dead man, again and again brushing her hand over his hair, until led away from the coffin. Meanwhile various Politburo Members, visibly relaxed and unconcerned, were putting their heads together for prolonged discussions. The message to the Soviet public was, as one British newspaper put it: "Look, this is a personal loss, but not a political one."

The new man's style of management was felt that same afternoon by the foreign heads of state and government who were welcomed and received by Gorbachev. With him was the 75-year-old Foreign Minister Andrei Gromyko, who had supported the new Kremlin leaders during the two previous changes of power. But now it was Gromyko who suddenly looked in need of support.

Gorbachev, calm, self-assured and competent, spoke freely with only an occasional glance at the documents lying before him. Talking to the West European heads of state and government, he consistently pursued his dual strategy against President Reagan's space plans. He accused France's President Mitterrand, Mrs. Thatcher and the German Chancellor, Helmut Kohl, of ranging themselves too unquestioningly on America's side (he even accused Kohl of standing to attention before Ronald Reagan). Yet at the same time — more strongly than Chernenko a year before or Andropov a little over two years before — Gorbachev emphasised the importance of good bilateral relations. The West European leaders were clearly impressed by the new Party chief. Mitterrand said that Gorbachev had "a relaxed, resolute mind ... totally unpolemical." Kohl called the Kremlin leader a man of "natural authority" and with "remarkable command of the subject"; he had "spoken with concentration and decisiveness."

Not much later the American Vice-President George Bush, talking in the White House to a West German politician, warned him that Gorbachev was an "impressive ideas salesman." Implicit in Bush's remark was the concern that Gorbachev's declarations on the theme of peace might be more effective than those of the Old Guard in impressing Europe. Great care had to be taken therefore lest Gorbachev's eloquent declarations should widen the gulf between Europe and the United States.

Which was exactly Gorbachev's aim — to prevent new treaties between European governments and the White House about participation in President Reagan's space defence initiative. His main reason for wishing to foil the American plans was (and still is) his need for a relaxation of economic pressure, so that he has the time and money to reorganize the Soviet Union internally and modernize its structures.

But how much can he achieve against the lethargy and backwardness of the old ways? Others before him have tried and failed. A glance at past attempts at reform offers interesting parallels with Gorbachev's current plans. No direct comparison is intended, but it is instructive to see how radical minds have been crushed by the sheer dead weight of Russia's problems.

2
The Burden of the Past

Mikhail Gorbachev, from the moment of his accession, stormed the ramparts of Soviet bureaucracy, announcing his determination to tackle the most intractable problems and exhorting common citizens and officials alike to lend a hand. Yet the new General Secretary is faced with a dilemma to which no reformer has ever found a solution. In order to raise their country's power and prestige, its military technology and economic efficiency, its public health and education to the level of the more highly developed West, reformers have invariably appealed to the people's diligence and sense of community. But the very idea of the people participating in legislation is alien to Russia's autocratic traditions. Participation has never been widely discussed, and indeed has frequently been illegal. Consequently, if autocratic power fails, there has never been anything but empty ritual to take its place.

Gorbachev's problems are often described as those of Soviet Russia; in fact, 1917 marked less of a break than its leaders like to believe. The problems he faces are in many ways comparable to the problems of the remoter past. To understand them, it is as well to look back not decades, but centuries, beginning with Peter the Great (1672–1725).

Peter the Great, the first and perhaps the greatest of those leaders ambitious for reform, was incessantly urging on his lethargic compatriots. Whenever a fire broke out in the city — a frequent occurrence in Moscow in the early 18th century — the Tsar himself would take charge of the fire-fighting. "Being endowed with an exceptionally quick intelligence," the Danish envoy, Just Juel, reported, "the Tsar sees at once what needs to be done to contain the fire. He climbs up on the roof, moves to the most dangerous spots, encourages people and nobles alike to lend a hand, and does not rest until the fire is out. If, however, the ruler is not present, things are totally different. Then the people just watch, often with total indifference, and no one helps. It is entirely useless to berate them or to offer them money to help; they merely wait for the moment when they can steal something."

Juel pinpointed an inherent fault in Russian society — the connection between domestic backwardness and imperial drive, between public indifference and absolute autocracy. That they remained so intimately connected was the consequence of the irresistible growth of the tsarist and Soviet empires. In 1300, the Principality of Moscow covered an area of only 20,000 square kilometres (about 7,700 square miles). During the next 150 years, it grew more than twenty-fold. By 1600, immediately prior to the conquest of Siberia, the Muscovite empire was already as large as the rest of Europe. By its conquest of Siberia in the mid-17th century, the tsarist empire became the largest state in the world.

Moreover, more than any other European dynasty, the rulers of Russia equated political power with territorial growth and the absolute rule of the landowner — a rigid system not in tune with an international order based on a balance of power, the kind of order evolving under their aristocratic cousins in Western Europe. Only military confrontation with the West made Russia's rulers realize the backwardness of their country.

Peter the Great was the first to try to remould Russia. To his predecessors, territorial growth had meant everything and the education of the serfs had meant nothing. Peter wished to transform this system, to imbue it with a dynamic spirit that would sweep the people along. Specifically, he aimed to overtake the West in military terms. To do this, he needed men with military skills. This need led to the creation of a system of public education. Until then, mass ignorance had been regarded as a proper consequence of the gulf fixed between commoners and rulers. Now that gulf became somewhat less fixed. Even though the Tsar's gigantic schemes concentrated chiefly on military skills, he aimed to achieve something much more wide-ranging. Wishing to exact as much as possible from all strata of society, he saw that productivity could not be achieved without a freer flow of information. Within a comparable framework of absolutism, Peter believed what Gorbachev proclaimed upon his accession: "The better informed a person is, the more responsibly will he work." So that his subjects should learn about events in the rest of the world, the Tsar even decreed that a news-sheet be published in Moscow: *Vedomosti*, the first Russian newspaper.

And there was something else Peter was the first to realize: the deeply devout attitude of the people, which to his predecessors seemed to reflect their own Byzantine omnipotence, also resulted in a dull indifference which led his subjects to reject all responsibility and personal initiative. "Less subservience!" he proclaimed, "More zeal in service and more loyalty to me and the state — that is the respect that should be paid to the Tsar!"

Unlike his predecessors, Peter did not rule from behind the Kremlin walls, with his subjects' petitions and pleas for mercy being hoisted up in a basket. Nor did he, like most of his 20th-century successors, hide behind the curtains of his state coaches. This tsar reigned from coach and saddle, from sleigh and ship. He was an indefatigable traveller. He made inspections and issued decrees. Yet, for all his restlessness, he never found any way to escape his own absolutism by delegating responsibility.

It was only the challenge from the West that led to a slight slackening of centralized autocracy. When in 1708

Sweden's King Charles XII moved against Russia with an army that was reputedly invincible, Peter hurriedly moved to decentralize the administration. Russia was divided into eight huge governmental districts. Their governors were granted the power to recruit soldiers and collect taxes. The result was chaos — a hopeless confusion of decrees, information and income. To his close collaborator Menshikov, one of the new governors, Peter wrote: "We know no more about your administration than about that of a foreign country."

Peter was as zealous, and as unsuccessful, in his assault on another major problem: corruption. In 1713, all subjects were ordered to report to Peter without delay any instance of corruption in their area. As a result of this campaign, a chain of corruption was revealed that reached all the way up to the highest level of government. Then as now the problems of transport offered rich pickings. Every village had to provide food for the army and deliver it to the towns, even in the remote newly conquered regions. The transportation was organized by middlemen who, in return for their services, retained part of the supplies. Inquiries revealed that numerous nobles and officials were arranging these deliveries under assumed names. Investigations extended to Peter's closest collaborators much as they did to Brezhnev's clan, except that, unlike Brezhnev, the Tsar personally supported the investigations. Prince Menshikov, Prince Gagarin (Governor of Siberia), the Vice-Governor of St. Petersburg, the Chief of Artillery and the Director of the Admiralty were all among those who had to answer for themselves before a commission. The highest government representatives escaped with heavy fines; senior officials were publicly flogged, mutilated or banished; some of the accused were hanged.

In his fight against corruption, Peter even appointed 500 public prosecutors, or "fiscals," as permanent representatives of the law. The most zealous prosecutor, and one soon hated at Court and in the Church, was Alexei Nesterov. As Supreme Fiscal, he had his own son prosecuted, and overthrew Gagarin, who, in spite of his meritorious service, was publicly hanged. Then, after ten years of indefatigable investigation, Nesterov himself was found guilty of corruption, and beheaded. Corruption did not, of course, die with him. As the Tsar once put it, public money was "running out of everyone's sleeves."

Internationally, his achievements were indisputable. After 21 years of military conflict, as he himself said, "We have, through our feats in war, risen from darkness into the light of the world, and those in the light, whom we did not know, now have respect for us." But what of his efforts to establish the foundations of a productive society, what of his hopes of leading the population from technological backwardness into the modern age? The answer was given at the time by Peter's admirer Ivan Pososhkov: "Here the mighty monarch makes the greatest effort and yet he achieves nothing; he has few helpers; with ten men he pulls a load uphill, but millions lean against it: how then can his work progress?"

How indeed? Even his fire-fighting efforts were wasted, ironically because they were so successful. As a tribute to his exemplary work, later tsars were impelled by tradition to indulge in ritualized visits to Moscow fire-brigades.

As Peter the Great had tried to raise Russia's army, industry and crafts to the level of that of the West, Catherine the Great endeavoured to do the same with Russia's public health, education and judiciary. While Peter had built better hospitals for his soldiers, Catherine II founded hospitals for the civilian population. In some respects, her achievements were unparalleled in all Europe. She founded a five-storey foundlings' home in Moscow, along with a maternity hospital and a dairy farm with 80 cows. The foundlings' home accepted 2,000 children annually. Mothers wishing to accommodate their new-born babies in this home had only to ring the bell, whereupon a small basket was lowered. The mother laid the baby in the basket, which was then hoisted up again. If a child was found to be gifted, it received free schooling up to secondary school level. The Moscow foundlings' home became a model for smaller homes in five other Russian cities.

Catherine also initiated some unusual measures to fight epidemics. She founded a 60-bed hospital exclusively for those suffering from venereal diseases. The patients were allowed to remain anonymous. Where Peter had invited Western craftsmen, merchants and technicians to Russia, Catherine brought in English specialists to check the spread of smallpox, setting an example by having herself and 140 St. Petersburg nobles vaccinated. While Peter, on Leibniz's advice, had set up Russia's Academy of Sciences, Catherine in 1763 founded Russia's first medical college.

Catherine, born in Germany in 1729, four years after Peter's death, did not confine herself to individual spectacular projects merely to impress Europe. She also tried, in a country that had no schools, to build up a system of simple elementary education. Advised by Austrian and English pedagogues, she issued the first educational decree for the whole of Russia. Each provincial capital was to have a higher school with six teachers. For each district town an elementary — or "people's" — school was envisaged with two teachers. They were called People's Schools because "all subjects of Her Imperial Majesty may now receive an education that is appropriate to their estate."

For the upper classes, Catherine encouraged the study of Western culture, or more accurately of Greco-Roman antiquity and of contemporary Western Europe. The world of Homer, Plato, Ovid and Cicero — a world until then virtually unknown in Russia — was opened up. Contemporary European literature, from Goethe's *Werther* to *Gulliver's Travels*, was published in translation. Catherine, unlike her tsarist and communist successors, even had the principal writings on human rights — above all Montesquieu — translated. The Empress herself wrote satires and comedies, fairy-tales and essays on Russian history (though most of her writings were dull and moralizing, not unlike the products churned out by Brezhnev's and Chernenko's ghost writers).

Russians under Catherine were freer to discuss moral and social topics than ever before. Just as Peter tried to

impose his innovations on his unwilling compatriots, so
Catherine endeavoured to lead the thinking of the country
she loved — but had remarkably little lasting impact. Such
a task exceeded not only her strength but also the limits
set by autocracy.

Take, for example, the issue of serfdom. The youthful
Catherine believed that it "offends against all justice and
the Christian religion that men born free like all others
should be made slaves." Influenced by Montesquieu's *Spirit of the Laws*, she made it her aim to abolish serfdom and
to struggle against the various forms of oppression in the
country. And she did indeed manage to alleviate the worst
effects of serfdom. She rescinded a regulation under which
foundlings, illegitimate children and orphans became serfs
of those who took them in. She forbad landowners from
re-enslaving a manumitted serf. And she laid down the
conditions under which a landowner had to give a serf his
freedom. She even opened up her new schools to serfs and
enabled them — at least on paper — to enter university. In
this connection she proclaimed: "The sciences are called
liberal so that they should give everyone the liberty to
acquire them and not that this right should be restricted to
those free already."

Her efforts, however, produced conflicting results, as
most attempted reforms in Russia have done. In spite of
Catherine's proclamations, serfdom in Russia reached its
highest point in her reign, being extended into the
Ukraine. From her famous *Instruction to the Commission
for Preparing a Project of a New Code of Laws,* her aristocratic collaborators expunged everything that even re-
motely touched upon the issue of rural serfdom. Catherine
was unable to get to the root of the evil because in doing so
she would have encountered the head-on resistance of the
nobility.

No sovereign ever criticized the system itself in the way
Catherine did. In one of her letters from the 1760's, she
wrote: "Voltaire, my master, forbids the prediction of the
future because those who do so are fond of constructing
systems, and the builders of systems pack into them what-

ever fits and whatever does not fit, whatever is right and whatever is not right; and finally love of self becomes love of the system, which gives rise to obduracy, intolerance and persecution — threats against which my master has warned me."

Fine words, but empty ones. Voltaire's and Montesquieu's disciple she may have been, but she did not deserve the halo she enjoyed in Europe. The fact is that Catherine time and again put "reasons of state" above the reason of the Enlightenment. She was herself a constructor of systems — an imperial system under which Russia increasingly packed into her growing territory "whatever fits and whatever does not fit." It was Catherine who decided to wipe Poland off the map. What Peter had done in the North she did in the South. He achieved access to European waters via the Baltic; she made a grab for the Black Sea, creating a sea-route to Europe by the back door. In 1794, as Catherine's biographer Vincent Cronin records, the British ambassador reported "a new chart of the Russian Empire, in which a considerable tract of the North West Coast of America (as far as Vancouver) is found to be part of Her Imperial Majesty's Dominions."

All in all, what with Poland, the Black Sea coast, the Crimea and the coast of Alaska — territories equal to the size of France, with seven million inhabitants — Russia's population increased from 19 to 29 million in her 34-year reign.

With such a territorial gain and an increase in population, Catherine's zealous plans for education all but sank without trace. At the time of her death, there were only 316 state schools, with 744 teachers, 16,220 boy and 1,121 girl pupils. Some 97 percent of the Russian people were still illiterate. Until well into the next century, state expenditure on education amounted to about one-fifth of the maintenance costs of the imperial family and the Court. As a non-Russian, Catherine won more sympathy among the St. Petersburg nobility and the country's scattered elite by enlarging the national territory than by reducing oppression, and found her bold ideas sadly shipwrecked. She had to place her hopes of an early end to serfdom in her grandson Alexander.

Alexander I, whom Catherine had called "my legacy to Russia," ascended the throne in 1801, at the age of 23. Because of his comparatively liberal education, guided by his grandmother, it was expected that he would be a decisive reformer. And he made a promising start. During the first years of his reign, Alexander banned the sadistic forms of corporal punishment that dated from darker periods. He took a few steps to ease the conditions of the serfs. He even modified the traditionally cumbersome administrative apparatus. Yet Catherine's grandson, brought up in the spirit of 18th-century rationalism, was afraid of the logical consequences of his cautious reforms — the introduction of democratic rights. The ingrained autocrat in him prevailed over the enlightened intellectual.

Alexander, too, decided that he would rather enhance his reputation by foreign adventures. Against the advice of his generals, he pursued Napoleon's army all the way into Western Europe and in March 1814 entered Paris. He had himself hailed as Europe's liberator from despotism and proposed a Holy Alliance of conservative European monarchies to the Emperor of Austria and the King of Prussia. Yet while he was offering counsel to the West, declaring himself in favour of self-determination, he withheld any further independence from his Russian subjects. He allowed his financial reforms — for the taxation of great landowners and the creation of a properly regulated public budget — to peter out, increasingly abandoning himself to religious mysticism. In the end, he left domestic administration in the hands of a reactionary bureaucracy.

One tsar did risk the leap towards granting greater freedom, only to scramble back to safety again. Alexander II in 1861 proclaimed the abolition of serfdom, for which he became known both as "the Liberator" and also as the most controversial figure among the last rulers of the Old Russia.

As tsarevich, Alexander visited Siberia for seven months in 1837, the first Romanov to do so. To the despair of his officials, the 19-year-old heir to the throne spontaneously entered wretched hovels; saw the sufferings of chained convicts in punitive settlements; and visited the Decembrists, whom his father Nicholas I had sent into exile after their abortive rising in 1825. The young man despatched a special courier back to the capital and obtained permission to have the exiles' lot made easier. With these experiences behind him, the young Alexander fully understood his country's backwardness.

But it soon became clear that even he — uncertain what the weakening of autocracy might bring — could not delegate any responsibility for his huge task. When a few well-meaning nobles wanted to share in the business of government, offering to do so without any financial reward, Count Valuyev, the Interior Minister, replied in a circular that the Assemblies of Nobles were to confine themselves to their local problems. Under no circumstances were they to voice opinions or make recommendations on government matters.

Alexander, too, compensated for internal vacillation with yet another expansionist drive, with huge gains of territory in the east and south, and a tough policy of assimilation in the west (where the Poles responded to his liberal concessions with demands for yet greater liberties). "The Liberator" enlarged the empire by 2.5 million square kilometres (about 965,000 square miles), an expansionist move that included pacifying the Caucasus by giving the 400,000 Circassians an ultimatum: they had ten weeks to make up their minds whether they would move into the Russian steppe or emigrate to Turkey (they chose Turkey, leaving the western Caucasus empty and desolate).

By the early 20th century, the pattern of Russian history was well established. The tsars, whether they acted as barbarian despots or as humane reformers, always increased Russian territory, and always relied on autocracy to guarantee imperial strength, regardless of social suffering. This was the legacy the Soviets were to inherit.

Before they came into their inheritance, one last reformer of the old empire took the stage: Peter Stolypin, the head of government from 1906. His aim was to let the peasants develop in their own way, by promoting market relations and the growth of private property. Under Stolypin's 1906 legislation, a peasant could leave his commune at any time he wished. The lands that until then had belonged to members of the imperial family could now be purchased on credit by small rural producers through the Farmers' Bank. The impoverished and neglected communal systems of landholding were to disappear. The reform introduced the concept of productivity into Russian agricultural economy, with the aim of establishing groups of independent farming enterprises, no longer dependent on one another.

As usual, the reforms had little effect, for several reasons. The extensive land ownership by the nobility remained unchanged; there was thus little land the peasants could actually acquire. Many peasants, unwilling to face the risks entailed in running their own smallholdings, were violently opposed to leaving the communes (a point worth emphasizing because of the Western belief, now virtually stereotyped, that collectivization by the communists was and still is the only obstacle to a flourishing agriculture in Russia. No question that Stalin's war against the peasantry wrecked Soviet agriculture, but it had no great strength in the first place). And finally, the peasants were too poor to benefit from the reforms. In contrast to Western Europe then and to the Soviet Union today, the social result of industrialization in Russia was not the emergence of a poor urban proletariat, but rather the pauperization of much of the peasantry, who stayed on the land in ever more wretched conditions.

Something of the pre-Revolutionary problems carries through to the present; but the turmoil of the Revolution and the years that followed created a new set of problems that were the consequence of inadequate, often brutal attempts to solve previous difficulties. Those years have left a legacy of bitterness, suspicion and chronic inefficiency that today's reformers will find hard to overcome.

The fate of the October Revolution was decisively affected by the 1918—1920 Civil War. Industries, facing demands which greatly exceeded their capacity, produced fewer and fewer consumer goods. In response, the peasants supplied less and less of their produce to the industrial centres. Exchange of commodities between town and country petered out, and the industrial workers, in particular, were faced with a worsening famine.

In May 1918, the communist leadership embarked on a food policy rigidly dictated from above. The People's Commissariat for Food Supplies was given full powers to compel the peasants to surrender their produce. Since industrial production was switched to military equipment and the state's bulk buyers of grain were less and less able to offer the peasants agricultural implements, hardware or textiles in exchange for their grain, the buyers increasingly had to resort to force. Even the "Committees of Village Poor," the supposed allies of the Revolution who had begun by requisitioning the grain stocks of the more affluent peasants, the kulaks, more and more frequently retained the confiscated stocks in the villages instead of delivering them to the towns. The urgent need for food in the Red Army and the industrial centres eventually resulted in quotas being imposed even on the poorer peasants.

As conditions in towns became increasingly intolerable and communist rule more and more ruthless, a wave of revolt swept through nearly all the rural areas which had to deliver foodstuffs. In Tambov, 240 miles south-east of Moscow, some 30,000 rebellious peasants united into an army. For weeks, peasant armies in western Siberia blocked all communications to European Russia. The Volga region and the Ukraine were rocked by disturbances. Resistance reached its peak in February 1921 with a mutiny of the garrison in Kronstadt, the naval base of the Baltic Fleet just outside Petrograd (as Leningrad was then called). The men — as in all subsequent risings against the

Soviet system, including the Polish strikes of August 1980
— began by making material demands and went on to
political ones: new elections to the soviets and freedom for
all socialist organizations. Russia's new reformers had
rapidly come up against their limits.

Lenin drew a parallel between the Bolsheviks in the
1920's and the Jacobins during the French Revolution. The
Bolsheviks, like the Jacobins, found further revolutionary
terror and economic centralization intolerable. The Bolsheviks, he decided, could save themselves only if they were
prepared for a drastic revision of their past policy. In
March 1921, while the Kronstadt mutiny was in progress,
the 10th Congress of the Soviet Communist Party decided
to replace the peasants' quotas by a levy in kind that was
substantially lower. The peasants were allowed to dispose
freely of any surpluses left in their hands. The "New Economic Policy" (NEP) was born, restoring to the peasants
and small tradesmen the right to develop their own
businesses. A further decree allowed the state to lease
small enterprises to private individuals. By the beginning
of 1922, more than 10,000 such enterprises had been
assigned, creating a type of communism in which craftsmen and peasants could once more be responsible for their
own income.

The New Economic Policy has remained something of a
point of controversy in all Soviet discussions on reform,
providing a historical arena in which supporters and opponents of private initiative clashed. Recently, Andropov and
Gorbachev have once again presented the NEP as an example of a courageous search for solutions to crises. This
was a much more controversial issue than some Western
observers believed, as was revealed in 1984 by a sharp
dispute about the NEP between two influential Moscow
periodicals engaged in an unusually fierce exchange. In
Questions of History a social scientist, Yevgeni Ambarzumov, summarized the mutiny of the Kronstadt garrison
and Lenin's conclusions from it, and went on to analyse the
tensions which had appeared in the Eastern Bloc, from

Hungary in 1956 to Poland in 1980. He no longer described these as "counter-revolutionary crises" but, surprisingly, as "sociopolitical crises." Lenin's NEP, he claimed, had been the best strategy at the time, "not liberalism, but profound political realism." It is clear that, by invoking Lenin (and with support from Gorbachev), the author was pleading for far-reaching structural changes, simultaneously defending them against the objections of the planning bureaucrats.

"That strategy [of Lenin] was most serious and no easy matter," he wrote. "It marked, in many respects, a far-reaching turning point: in the political line, in the slogans, in working methods, in the selection of cadres. Yet, as history has shown, it proved successful all along the line. The New Economic Policy, introduced in order to resolve a crisis, developed into an optimal strategy for the transition to communism."

The present-day lessons which Ambarzumov derived from it revealed even more clearly the violence of the discussions behind the scenes: "The contemporary experience of overcoming bottlenecks in many socialist countries, achieved with the help of small-scale proprietors from various groups, confirms Lenin's forecast and refutes the jealous guardians of purity and their unjustified clinging to projects that may be correct in theory but are unrealizable in practice."

The deputy editor-in-chief of *Kommunist*, Yevgeni Bugayev, replied — and in doing so revealed the still rigid positions of the planning bureaucracy. The lessons of the NEP period, he said, were no longer relevant today. Ambarzumov was idealizing private enterprise although it ran counter to the forms of socialist collectivism and resulted in unjustified disparitites in wages. Moreover, Ambarzumov had nowhere mentioned those right-wing opportunists who had prepared the counter-revolution — like Nagy in Hungary and Dubček in Czechoslovakia.

In point of fact — to return once more to Lenin's time — the

NEP was by no means an unqualified success. Since the state and the towns were still unable to offer sufficient industrial goods to the peasants, the peasants' interest in selling their produce soon declined. They fed more and more of their grain to their livestock and hoarded their produce. Clearly, even Lenin's resort to market economies utterly failed to prevent dramatic new upheavals in market relationships.

Moreover, the recovery of agriculture restored differences among the peasantry. In the poor Russian villages, where sowing was still done by hand and reaping by sickle, the few rich peasants, the kulaks, had an advantage.

In the late 1920's, communist propaganda described the peasantry as divided into three parts like Caesar's Gaul (as the historian Adam B. Ulam states in his biography *Stalin, The Man and his Era*, the conclusions of which are summarized here). There were the village poor; there were the middle peasants who were able to feed themselves and their families; and there were the ten percent who were class enemies, the kulaks. There were those in high positions who asked: Was the NEP not now strengthening those class enemies? What had happened to socialism and industrialization? These were questions around which the struggle for power raged.

That struggle was eventually won by Stalin, whose answer was the First Five-Year Plan — a death sentence for millions and one of the greatest disasters ever to befall the Soviet Union.

In the spring of 1929 the delegates to the 5th Soviet Congress ecstatically crowded around a map on which gigantic industrial projects were marked. "Before our eyes lay our country as it would be in five years from now," *Pravda* enthused. "What inspiring perspectives! As though by a magic hand, the curtains which veil the future have been pulled aside. The enthusiasm of the delegates found its spontaneous expression in a mighty singing of the Internationale."

Yet the Internationale was in fact a farewell to internationalism, to Trotsky's permanent revolution. The Party

activists were cheering Stalin's "construction of socialism
in one country," his great leap forward, which was intended to catapult the backward Soviet empire into the
technological age. In 1929 Stalin announced: "If the development of our collective and state farm economy proceeds at a heightened pace then there is no reason to doubt
that our country in, say, three years will become one of the
most grain-rich countries, if not the most grain-rich country in the world." More realistically, and downright
prophetically as if he had a premonition of the German
attack of 1941, the Georgian despot announced in 1931:
"We are lagging behind the advanced countries by fifty or a
hundred years. We must close that gap in ten years. Either
we achieve this or we shall be crushed."

In a way, it was successful. The productivity of Soviet
industry, built up in the Russian hinterland at the expense
of agriculture in the 1930's, was totally underestimated by
Hitler.

But there is another, darker side to the Five-Year Plan.
Between 1928 and 1933, Russia's already pitiful standard
of living dropped by as much as one-third. Forced collectivization severed the peasantry, about 80 percent of the
population, from its scanty but ancient traditions. Millions
were deported, millions died in the famine resulting from
this vast transformation. The full extent of the tragedy,
buried in inaccessible Soviet archives, is still unresear-
ched. But there is no dispute about the verdict: Stalin's
"great leap" led to one of the great traumas of modern
history.

To the Bolsheviks, who despised the old rural Russia, it
seemed reasonable to use mechanization and large-scale
agricultural enterprises to obtain from the 25 million
peasant households the manpower needed for the factories
that were being planned. It was likewise clear to every
communist that the capital for the development of industry
would have to be squeezed out of the peasants, since the
hoped-for Western credits had failed to materialize after
the Civil War. Reasonable arguments, to hard-line Bolsheviks; but applied by methods that went far beyond the

bounds of reason. In retrospect, it is almost impossible to understand the obsessive hostility with which Stalin and his Party assaulted rural Russia. It was as if they held the peasants in superstitious dread, seeing them as denizens of a realm of darkness that had to be destroyed before modern industry could be built up.

The particular objects of Stalinist venom were the kulaks. In November 1929 Stalin announced: "We have recently embarked on the liquidation of the kulaks as a class." Kulaks resisting expropriation were shot or packed off to concentration camps. Others were deported in huge numbers to the Siberian mines. Others still were given a patch to farm, outside the collective farm system, and there, without the means to produce anything much, they eked out a wretched livelihood. That was the fate of approximately 4.5 million people.

The result of this manic onslaught was the total disintegration of agricultural production. A middle peasant, for example, would risk death if he overproduced, since that might result in his reclassification as a kulak. Other peasants, driven in large numbers into the collective farms, killed off their draught animals in protest. At the start of the 1928 Five-Year Plan the Soviet Union had 32 million horses, at its end it had scarcely more than 15 million. Cattle stocks declined from 60 to 33 million.

Mikhail Sholokhov described these protest slaughterings in his novel *Virgin Soil Upturned*: "As soon as dusk fell one could hear the short-lived bleating of the sheep, the death squeals of the pigs and the mooing of the calves. Both individual peasants and those who had joined the collective farm were slaughtering everything.... The dogs were dragging offal through the village, the cellars were overflowing with meat. 'Slaughter them — they are no longer our animals!' These were the whispered words. They ate till they could eat no more .... Everybody was hiccuping and blinking like owls — intoxicated with food."

"Paper collectives" sprang up as local activists outdid each other in reporting successes. Yet according to the secret files of the Smolensk Party organization, which fell into the hands of the German occupiers, numerous Party brigades did their expropriating under the slogan: "Drink, eat — it's all ours now." Thus — as in Gogol's *Dead Souls* — a whole system of deception and self-deception was created. To this day production orders, and indeed entire factories, are discovered which exist only on paper, and which have enriched a whole chain of corrupt officials.

Worse was to come. In the winter of 1932–33, a famine broke out which cost at least four million lives. Nevertheless Stalin again ordered 1.7 million tonnes of grain to be exported. Today, by contrast, the Kremlin spends one-half of its hard currency on imports and foodstuffs. This proves, on the one hand, the extent to which the present leadership has departed from Stalin's methods and, on the other, that Soviet agriculture has still not recovered from Stalinism.

One other legacy of the famine stands in the way of Gorbachev's efforts to introduce a greater measure of personal initiative. For decades, the peasants have been punished for showing initiative. Now they are wary. The late critic of the regime, Andrei Amalrik, who was banished to a Siberian collective, wrote of this attitude in his book *Unwilling Journey to Siberia*. "They have not the slightest idea of how much an egg, a litre of milk or a kilogramme of pork costs them.... They indulge in the pleasant belief that they get something for nothing. They value their own labour just as cheaply as the collective and the state do."

Agriculture was sacrificed on the altars of Stalin's industrialization. These were monumental altars: the metallurgical plants of Magnitogorsk and Kuznetsk, the Turkestan-Siberian railway, the Volga-White Sea shipping canal, the gigantic Dnieper dam — altogether 1,500 large-scale projects. By means of rigid central control, and armies of slaves, Stalin succeeded in building his industrial base.

Yet the performance of these giants has remained exceptionally low to this day. The infamous lorry works on the Kama, whose launch in the 1970's was endlessly delayed, was a distant descendant of the Stalingrad tractor plant which, after only one year of construction, went into production in 1930. Stalin's colleague Grigori Ordzhonikidze later recalled: "When the plant was opened we produced a tractor in the summer. But then four or five months passed without our being able to produce another tractor or even spare parts."

The fact was that Stalin could impose his will on people but not on production figures. The original target of collectivization was overfulfilled many times. But many of the unrealistic targets for industry were not reached even years after the end of the First Five-Year Plan. The frenzy of printing money and then using it to build industry led to the collapse of the entire financial and credit system. Most enterprises simply ceased to calculate profit and loss.

The end of the First Five-Year Plan was described by the writer Vladimir Tendryakov in his novel *Death*: "In Vokhrovo, the district town, the peasants de-kulakized in the Ukraine would lie down to die in the little park by the railway station. People had got used to seeing the dead bodies there in the morning; a cart would stop and the stable-boy from the hospital, Abram, would load them up.... That was 1933."

The Soviet Union is still suffering from the consequences of Stalin's war against his own nation, in spite of the abandonment of mass terror and the moves towards mass consumption. As in wartime, the civilian economy is kept going by a black market and illegal barter. In order to implement unrealistic central planning, a factory manager will find some vital, unobtainable screw, the trouble-shooter who, like a Gogol character, has in fact been created by a planning system that cannot, with all its directives and bureaucratic channels, provide the spares, the manpower or the working morale that the economy needs.

The origins of this mess were touched upon by an important document, the Novosibirsk Research Paper of 1983. This document, produced by the Siberian branch of the Academy of Sciences, described the Moscow system of central planning as "incredibly compromised and outdated."
Academy of Sciences, described the Moscow system of central planning as "incredibly compromised and outdated."

"The basic features of the existing system of economic management," it said, "were created some 50 years ago.... There has never been a qualitative change to reflect the fundamental change in the state of productive forces."

Politically and socially, this is the world — a world of inefficiency and corruption rooted in Russian history — with which Gorbachev has to deal.

3

Steps on the Ladder of Success

The Caucasus, Gorbachev's homeland, consists of two parallel mountain ranges, the higher one in the south, the lower one in the north. Only two passes lead through these massive walls, known to Romans as the Caucasian Gates and the Caspian Gates, and now as the Darial and Derbent passes. In popular parlance, the Derbent Pass is also known as the "Gate of Alexander," for according to Caucasian tradition, Alexander the Great, in his battles against the Persian King Darius, was also faced by Caucasian and Armenian armies. Subsequently, many peoples have swept into the Caucasus — Alani and Goths, Avars and Huns, Persians, Mongols and Turks — driving defeated tribes and settlers deep into the Caucasian foothills and highland valleys. Only in the last century was this picturesque land finally subdued, by the Russians.

Where the lower range, the Black Mountains, drops away towards the north, where the river Yegorlyk runs down from the highlands into a fertile grain-growing plain, in the District of Krasnogvardeysk, lies the village of Privolnoye ("Liberty": it was settled by manumitted serfs in the last century). In summer, large expanses of grain fields, interspersed here and there by fields of sunflower, colour the landscape around Privolnoye.

Here on March 2 1931, Mikhail Sergeevich Gorbachev was born. The brief biography released by the Soviet news agency Tass on March 11 1985, when he was elected to be the new Party chief, stated no more about his origins than that he was born "into a peasant family." Why this rather vague statement? It took more than six months for the official biography of the man who, ever since his accession, has been calling for more information and "transparency," to add a few more details. In the late autumn of 1985 a *Biographical Outline* of nine typewritten pages was published. Yet the entire period from Gorbachev's birth to his summons to Moscow was compressed into the first three pages. The new version states: "Gorbachev's parents were genuine peasants who had to earn their daily bread by the sweat of their brows. His grandfather was one of the founders and the chairman of a collective farm. His father, Sergei Andreevich, proved his mettle first as an agricultural mechanic and later as a frontline soldier in the Great Patriotic War. His competence in his job, his careful husbandry, his Party-inspired sense of justice and his personal modesty earned him universal respect. His mother, Maria Panteleevna, was and still is equally hard-working, and at the age of 74 refuses to leave her native village."

This text, at any rate, implies that Gorbachev's father is no longer alive. As to the question of how long he was able to follow his son's career, there have been conflicting versions current in Moscow, and no clarification was provided during Gorbachev's first year in office. According to the first, official, version Gorbachev worked as a combine operator's assistant as early as 1946. The combine operator himself, Soviet sources have hinted, was Mikhail's father. In the second version, Sergei Andreevich Gorbachev, like 20 million other Soviet citizens, did not survive the Second World War; and Gorbachev himself has provided some evidence for this. In early September 1985, on the occasion of a visit to Moscow by a delegation of US Senators, Gorbachev asked the American interpreter, Dimitri Zarechnak, where he had learned such excellent Russian. Zarechnak, born in Czechoslovakia, replied that his father came from the Carpathian region. Thereupon Gorbachev replied: "That's where I lost my father." But he did not explain when and under what circumstances this occurred.

Ever since Stalin shut himself up in the Kremlin, it has been the practice for top-level Soviet officials to conceal their origins and private lives almost completely from the public. Gorbachev could hardly overturn this tradition overnight, even though in the course of his first year in office, and during his visits to London, Paris and Geneva, he did let private remarks and personal details slip into his speeches and discussions.

From the time he arrived in Moscow in 1978 until his accession to power, Gorbachev would visit his mother in Privolnoye every year on the occasion of his birthday in March. He even made the 900-mile trip in March 1985, only a few days before his appointment as General Secretary. No official information exists on these private visits; not even the local *Stavropolskaya Pravda* recorded them. How many relations Gorbachev still has in the region is still officially undisclosed. Research indicates that Gorbachev has a brother. But there are no relatives who have been elevated by him to high office.

The Gorbachev family is of Russian origin, having lived for an unknown time in the northern Caucasus, which was not part of the old Russia. The climate there is mild, the landscape beautiful. There are spas like Kislovodsk and Mineralnye Vody. The region is a rich ethnic mix. Among those of Russian origin, some have acquired a reputation for arrogance; others, stimulated perhaps by the hotch-potch of peoples, are seen as imaginative, curious, outgoing and exuberant. Members of the Soviet elite suffering from asthma are not the only people who say that breathing is easier in the Caucasus.

Ever since the days of Boris Godunov in the late 16th century, the Russians had worked their way closer to the Caucasus. In 1772, Peter the Great penetrated as far as Derbent; Catherine the Great sent out Cossack families from the Volga and the Don to settle in the Northern Caucasus, and in 1785 created the Governorship of the

Caucasus. Stavropol, Gorbachev's first political base, was founded as a fortress in 1777, as Outpost No. 8 in a line of Cossack defences. From the former fortifications of the Military Administration, now the Komsomol Park, the lines of communications ran to Tiflis (present-day Tbilisi) in Georgia and Baku in Azerbaijan. These roads were still threatened, well into the last century, by wild highland tribes and by fanatical Muslim guerrillas waging holy war.

The prolonged war of conquest fired the Russians' imagination because the Caucasus possessed so much that the central Russian plain lacked. The land formed the backdrop in the writings of Lermontov, Pushkin and Tolstoy. They portrayed the Caucasus as a realm of boundless adventure, of fast-running rivers and savagely romantic mountain peaks capped by eternal snows, of amazingly courageous Muslims and warlike Christian Georgians — a world far removed from Russia, with its lethargic serfs, its corrupt officials, its ignorant and disputatious nobles.

The people of the Caucasus have preserved their traditional individuality — and their opposition to being absorbed into the Russian nation. It was this traditional wariness, not any feeling for Nazism, that led the Muslim minority of the Stavropol Region, the Karachais, to collaborate with the Germans, who in 1942 briefly occupied Stavropol (then named Voroshilovsk, after Stalin's former Defence Minister). The German Wehrmacht responded favourably to them by dissolving a few collective farms and permitting the private ownership of land, shops and cafes. Mikhail Suslov, who was later to become the country's leading ideologue and was then the local Party chief, found it impossible to organize any serious partisan resistance to the Germans. (He had his revenge: later he saw to it that the Karachais were deported.) Suslov is often described as an early patron of Gorbachev. But no exceptional tribute is nowadays paid to him in Stavropol: an irrigation canal bears his name and a memorial display in the airport building, unveiled in 1985 to mark the 40th anniversary of victory over Nazi Germany, shows him in a photograph, but that is all.

Gorbachev was ten when Hitler attacked the Soviet Union. Although no official information is available on the fate of his family during the war, the Gorbachevs were apparently not evacuated to the east at the time. As a student, Gorbachev would occasionally mention that as a child he helped with the harvest close to the front. This suggests that he shared the anxieties and hardships of the civilian population, even though his immediate area did not experience the Nazi terror or destruction to quite the same terrible degree as other parts of the Soviet Union.

On the other hand, Gorbachev was too young to have shared the formative experiences of the war. To the older generation, participation in the war had been a personal patriotic deed; and at the same time, in spite of all its frightful horrors, they had experienced the war as a rebirth. At the front, they had encountered more human comradeship than they ever did under Stalin's terror, which, towards the end of the 1930's, had poisoned all relationships.

After the war, Gorbachev carried on from where, as a boy, he had helped with the harvest. "At the age of 14 he already drove a combine harvester," the new *Biographical Outline* states, though in 1979 the local *Stavropolskaya Pravda* said that this had merely been a holiday job during the summer. According to the biography released by Tass on the day of his accession, Gorbachev had later been a "mechanic at a machine and tractor station." There is no mention of this in the more recent version of his biography, which merely says: "Mikhail Gorbachev completed his upper school with a silver medal."

The variation between such tiny details may seem trivial. But in a Soviet context they are not insignificant. The Kremlin leaders used to emphasize in their biographies their humble origins in order to legitimize themselves as rightful leaders in the dictatorship of the proletariat. These minor amendments to Gorbachev's biography seem to indicate that this representative of a more relaxed generation no longer regards it as quite so indispensable to insist that his youth was rooted in the class struggle.

In any event, the young man distinguished himself even in his early Stavropol days. At the age of 18 he received the "Red Banner of Labour Group" decoration, an unusual distinction for one so young. This award opened to him the most important door of his career. At the age of 19, on the recommendation of his municipality, he was sent to Moscow to study at the university. As a law student, he later liked to wear in his lapel the decoration that helped him get there.

Gorbachev now moved from a poor, somewhat limited rural community through impoverished and rubble-strewn cities to Moscow, the heart of Soviet power, where he would be close to that genius Stalin, who understood all the laws of mankind's development and made them work for his nation's good. What other spot on earth could have held out such promise to a 19-year-old from a village almost a thousand miles away? He already had his shining faith; soon he would also have knowledge. These were the lines along which virtually all young political activists thought — Komsomol members, students from working-class or peasant backgrounds, and the youngest graduates from Party high schools. The younger generation was still under the spell of Stalin's personality cult, unwittingly enmeshed by his bombast, lies and manias.

There was, however, no sign in Moscow's everyday life of a grand future when Gorbachev arrived in September 1950 for the beginning of the academic year. The Stromynka student hostel by Sokolniki Park, where he lodged, was a huge barracks, developed from military accommodation built by Peter the Great. The Soviet government had enlarged it by adding two additional floors, turning it into a home for nearly 10,000 students. Between seven and 15 students shared a dormitory. On each floor there was just a single communal toilet, a washroom and a kitchen.

Four years later, Gorbachev and his fellow-students moved into the new building of the Lomonosov State University on the Lenin Hills, a building that has since become the symbol of modern Moscow. Here every student had his own small modern room, sharing toilet and shower with only one other student. Given the conditions of the day this was a move into palatial luxury; and at a time of awakening, but still vague, doubts about Stalin's perfection, it was material evidence that the Soviet government was on the right road.

But even the cramped conditions of the Stromynka student hostel revealed a totally new and undreamed-of world for young provincials like Gorbachev. Here were fellow-students from all over the vast expanse of the Soviet Union, discussing different experiences and living conditions. There were the older students who, as boy-soldiers, had helped to chase the Germans beyond the frontiers of the Soviet Union and, in doing so, had discovered that Russia's neighbours were rather better off than they were themselves. And, above all, there were students from these neighbouring countries, newly brought into the socialist fold. They, too, did not doubt the wise leader in the Kremlin. But they were more discerning, with an acute eye for the backwardness of the Soviet Union.

What were such encounters like for a committed young Soviet citizen? Among Gorbachev's fellow-students during the five years of his Moscow studies was Zdenek Mlynar, the brightest of those who conceived the Czechoslovak Spring of 1968. In his book *Night Frost*, published in 1978, he describes a hostel discussion, the sort of exchange Gorbachev could well have experienced:

"On one occasion I was roused in the middle of the night by students from a nearby dormitory in order to settle a dispute. At issue was the question whether in the villages of Czechoslovakia the houses were really built of bricks (and not just of clay and timber) and roofed with real tiles (instead of straw). A former soldier, who had spent some time in Czechoslovakia towards the end of the war, claimed to have seen these things. Another student, who knew nothing of the world except his native collective farm and had come straight from it to Moscow, simply refused to believe it. The others in the room — perhaps ten people, all between 20 and 30 — were uncertain which of the two to side with. I confirmed the statement of the soldier who had seen the miracle with his own eyes. This put an end to the argument, but from the expression on the face of the chief opponent I gathered he was still not entirely convinced; he evidently suspected me of boastful patriotism."

However, the most important door into the world for an eager and inquisitive student like Gorbachev was his own subject. Law at that time was special in several respects. Until well into the 1960's, less than five percent of the students studied law or economics. Stalin's legal doctrine, of course, knew only one theorem: the law is whatever the state proclaims the law to be. And yet the faculty of law was the only one that was permitted to examine the origins of ideas about the state. Even if the interpretations were predictable, Gorbachev and his fellow-students at least heard and read things that would never reach the ears or eyes of other students: general constitutional law from Hammurabi to the present day, the history of political ideas, Machiavelli and Hobbes, Hegel and Rousseau. For one semester Gorbachev had to cram Latin. Even though he acquired no more than the most basic knowledge, at least he got to know a number of legal technical terms, the use of foreign words, and the Latin script.

Thus the gifted young man from Privolnoye, at an age when his learning capacity and receptivity were at their peak, was offered, and seized, a rare opportunity, such as had seldom been granted to the Party cadres of the previous generation and one that scarcely even existed for his own contemporaries under Stalin: the opportunity to gain an insight into a different political culture. It was partly his pursuit of legal studies that subsequently enabled him to move with such assurance in the West. Had he studied economics, or engineering, or science, or had he merely taken the more usual road for rising talent, namely to attend the Party high school for three years, he would have been denied much.

As for the world around him, Gorbachev viewed it realistically, in spite of his Marxist ideals. Mlynar to this day remembers his fellow-student's sober assessment of the situation in the countryside: "When we were studying collective farm law, Gorbachev explained to me how insignificant collective farm legislation was in day-to-day life and how important, on the other hand, was brute force, which alone ensured working discipline on the collective farms."

But "brute force" in his sense bore little relationship to the realities of Stalin's terror. Unless his own family had been affected by Stalin's purges, a young student would not usually discover about political terror through his law studies. Nor would he necessarily learn anything more in the course of his practical work. As a probationer in the public prosecutor's office, Gorbachev, like all his fellow-students, must have repeatedly witnessed interrogations in Moscow's prisons. Zdenek Mlynar, for instance, was present at numerous examinations in the notorious Lefortovo prison. He recalls in *Nightfrost*: "At that time I had no idea that in another wing of that institution the things were taking place which Solzhenitsyn has described. The Lefortovo prison is every bit as depressing as any other prison from the last century, but what I witnessed there was quite normal: examinations of criminal offenders were in accordance with the code of procedure. And these offenders did not give me the impression of persons unjustly detained or humiliated."

Many students, then, had no concept of the extent of Stalin's continuing terror. This applied less to students from the big cities, especially from Moscow, and more to new arrivals from the provinces. Cronid Lubarski, for instance, who now lives in Munich and who went to Moscow University a year after Gorbachev, knew a good deal about the nature and extent of the terror. But, he says, "there were many students who had no suspicion of it at all," adding that "if anyone wished to know more, he could certainly have found out." The fact was that many of them felt no such urge to discover the truth, and the things revealed by Khrushchev in 1956 were beyond their powers of imagination. This cannot be explained away as ideological blindness. The younger generation, especially the new elite in the universities, simply had no direct experience of the terror.

To them, the intrusiveness of the state showed itself in harmless, if often grotesque, ways. In the summer of 1951 Gorbachev went back to vacation in his village, where he again helped on the combine harvesters. One day the local police chief in person appeared among the crops. He had come to hand the student a highly suspect item of mail. It was a picture postcard from Prague, sent to Gorbachev by his new friend Zdenek Mlynar. It was suspect for no other reason than that it came from abroad.

In October 1952 Gorbachev joined the Communist Party. Although he did so while Stalin was still alive (and about to embark on his last great purge following the discovery of the so-called Doctors' Plot), there is nothing sinister about his timing. One did not have to be a zealot in order to join. During the war, and for some time afterwards, membership of the Party had greatly declined. In March 1949 the Party had only just over nine million members — roughly as many as before the war. An intensified enrolment campaign was launched in the early 1950's, and those joining the Party then were predominantly young people, like Gorbachev.

Was Gorbachev a Stalinist at that time? He was quite certainly a convinced follower of Stalin, one who expected the great father figure in the Kremlin to lead the Soviet people towards the ideals of communism with whatever firmness was needed. But equally certainly he was no bigoted fanatic, no spineless fawning careerist. According to Zdenek Mlynar, Gorbachev possessed a number of striking qualities. He was highly intelligent but not arrogant, loyal, honest and with a natural authority. He was a good listener. And finally he had the calm assurance of a man who had always tackled everything on his own and who, as a result, had gained the courage to oppose clearly whatever he considered to be wrong.

Mlynar has stories to support these impressions: "In 1952, we were studying the official history of the USSR, which required us to believe that anybody who deviated from an idea prescribed from above was thereby turning against the Party and must therefore be liquidated and expunged from history. Gorbachev commented to me: 'And yet, Lenin did not have Martov arrested but allowed him to emigrate.' This implied that Gorbachev doubted that people could be divided into two categories — those faithful to the official line, and criminals. He realized that there might be other groups as well, critics and reformers, who could not be classed as criminals. That he should have communicated this idea to someone else — moreover a foreign student — was quite exceptional. An opportunist would not have acted that way."

Mlynar is convinced that Gorbachev to this day retains the essence of what had then made him impressive: "To him, Marxist theory was not a collection of dogmas to be learned by rote; to him it had practical significance. I believe that, even after a lapse of 30 years, Gorbachev will not use that theory merely to win power. He is certain to realize today what power is and what practical politics are. But I think that politics and power are not goals in themselves for Gorbachev. He is no cynic. There is a lot of the reformer in his make-up. He regards politics as a means to an end, but his eyes are fixed on the end — human needs — not the means."

It is difficult to say whether, on the completion of his studies in Moscow, Gorbachev had privately turned his back on Stalin. Many did. Even the devout believers among the students experienced their first doubts about their idol when the Doctors' Plot dissolved into nothing and when in July 1953 Stalin's Secret Police chief Beria was arrested. Khrushchev's sensational Secret Speech at the 20th Party Congress in February 1956, in which he pilloried Stalin's crimes, is not likely to have come as a complete suprise to Gorbachev. But by then he was back in his native Stavropol.

He had left Moscow in 1955, having graduated from the Faculty of Law of the Lomonosov State University with distinction. He was accompanied to his native province by his wife Raisa Maksimovna Titorenko, a slim, strikingly attractive philosophy graduate (more accurately: a graduate of Marxism-Leninism), who had also lived in the Stromynka student hostel.

Gorbachev began his Party career — as did tens of thousands of his contemporaries — in the Komsomol, the communist youth organization. There was, however, one slight difference: very few of the young comrades who chose that road were lawyers. Gorbachev became Deputy Head of the Agitation and Propaganda Department in the Komsomol's Stavropol Regional Committee. Then in 1956, the year when de-Stalinization was started by Khrushchev, Gorbachev became secretary of the Komsomol in Stavropol. Two years later, he became First Secretary.

In March 1962 he switched over to the Party machine. By then he was 31. At first glance this no longer looked like a meteoric rise; countless similar careers ended right there, among colourless officials interested only in posts, benefits and privileges. But Gorbachev was different. He was quite unlike those old-style agit-prop officials who, after Party high school, sit behind green baize tables with their obligatory bottles of mineral water before them, issuing stereotyped appeals to the masses. Gorbachev was a novelty — a manager who took independent decisions and drew his own conclusions.

He became Party organizer for agriculture — to be exact, organizer of the Territorial Production Management of all Collective and State Farms in the Stavropol Region. Thus the trained lawyer for the first time moved into the field in which he was to make his career. He immediately took steps to discharge his new role more effectively by enrolling for a correspondence course at the Stavropol Institute of Agriculture. In 1967 he qualified as a "scientific agricultural economist."

That same year Raisa Gorbacheva, now 34, and the mother of a daughter named Irina, completed her doctoral thesis, forbiddingly entitled "Emergence of New Characteristics in the Daily Lives of the Collective Farm Peasantry (Based on Sociological Investigations in the Stavropol Region)." She submitted it to the V.I. Lenin Pedagogical Institute in Moscow. Her doctoral supervisor was the philosopher G.V. Osipov, a man who had opened new fields in Soviet sociology by developing various indicators for monitoring social trends.

In her investigations — according to her *Avtoreferat*, the summary that applicants must submit along with the thesis — Raisa had applied sociological methods that were then still very unusual in the Soviet Union. Her methods and sources included: firstly, official statistics, reports and analyses of regional Party and administrative bodies, and data from collective farms and communes; secondly, specific sociological investigations at five collective farms of different areas by participation and observation, personal interviews and conversations, as well as by questionnaire; and thirdly, documents from state archives of the Region, scientific publications, and verbal accounts by elderly rural inhabitants of traditional customs and attitudes.

Thus she employed anecdotal experience and empirical findings beyond the routine then customary. Moreover, she referred to a number of other theses — a very unusual practice in the Soviet Union to this day, either in doctoral theses or in scientific publications. Few doctoral researchers and social scientists work at such depth.

In addition, at a time when official philosophy still maintained that real-life processes could be moulded by ideology or were a reflection of ideology, Raisa Gorbacheva pursued a rather different route. This was evident even in the central theme of her thesis: "Difficulties and Contradictions" in the emergence of new features of rural life, and possible solutions.

Raisa Gorbacheva's doctoral thesis therefore provides some insights into living conditions at the very time — in the mid-1960's — when her husband was Party organizer for agriculture. The problems he had inherited, as her thesis shows, were considerable.

Although the Stavropol Region was regarded as developed, the 3,119 rural settlements, villages and farms had few services. The rural population, Raisa Gorbacheva calculated, was spending only one-fifth of what the urban population spent on those services. As late as 1965, she established, virtually all housing lacked such comforts as central heating, sewerage or a water supply, even though nearly one half of all collective farmers had moved into new or renovated houses since the mid-1950's. Real wage differentials were considerably greater than envisaged by official doctrine. Some collective farms were paying two to three roubles per working day, while others paid four or more.

As for the peasants' living conditions on the collective farms in the Stavropol Region, Raisa Gorbacheva concluded: "The material conditions of the collective farm peasantry are showing an upward trend." This was to put it at its most optimistic. The figures she cited now seem almost incredible. Thus in 1965 a rural dweller in the region spent on average only 3.46 roubles per month on the most indispensable services (footwear repairs, plumber, hairdresser, etc.), while an urban inhabitant even then would spend as much as 17.42 roubles — almost five times as much — on the same services. To draw a parallel with today (a rouble being worth about one pound): at present, a rural dweller in the Russian Republic spends approximately 30 roubles a month on such services, as against rather more than 40 roubles for the average urban dweller. According to the Statistical Annual for 1984, an industrial worker today earns 207 roubles per month on average. A collective farmer's wages — not separately listed in these statistics — is around 140 roubles per month. Employees in the educational or health services earn between 120 and 150 roubles.

Just 20 years ago — these astonishing differentials are revealed in the thesis — the average wage on the Stavropol collective farms (in 1964) was 33–50 roubles per month for unskilled labour, 83–117 roubles per month for skilled workers such as milkers, herdsmen, etc., and roughly 125

roubles per month for agricultural specialists. By presenting these facts Raisa Gorbacheva drew attention to a state
of affairs not accepted by Soviet sociological literature until very much later — that in terms of wages and education
"class differences" within one and the same class can be
greater than those between industrial workers and collective farmers.

Raisa Gorbacheva also cast some light on the development of the non-material side of living conditions in the
Stavropol Region. She provided data on the use made of
libraries and the frequency of cinema visits. And she
showed that notwithstanding a desire for education among
the rural population, they were still educationally backward. True, in the villages of Stavropol Region there was
practically no family left which did not have at least one
member who could read and write. The older generation,
however, still included a large number of illiterates. Raisa
adopted a statistical measure of educational standing, by
equating it with the ownership of icons. Of unskilled rural
labourer families, 66.6 percent owned icons at the time,
whereas among the "collective farm intelligentsia" only
16.6 percent did so. (Nowadays, icons are popular again,
though this has less to do with religion than with a desire
for ownership.)

By means of questionnaires, Raisa Gorbacheva also ex-
plored the collective farmers' leisure inclinations and attitudes. But her findings were not always in agreement with
the socio-political hopes and objectives of the Party. Of
course she referred to the Communist Party's guidelines,
but this merely highlighted the obstacles to further social
progress. One of the greatest problems, in her view, was
the position of rural women. That was why she emphatical-
ly drew the attention of the predominantly (male) Communist Party to the persistence of traditional attitudes: the
way men and women saw their own roles, and the division
of labour in the countryside which burdened the women
with most of the heavy physical work. She thus revealed a
fundamental contrast in the attitudes and the relationship
of the sexes between town and country.

Clearly, the quality of this thesis was well above the usual level, and points to a degree of enlightened thinking in both the author and her husband, who supported her research.

According to Marxist-Leninist concepts in the mid-1960's, the development of the socialist way of life was no longer solely determined by class characteristics but also by everyday experiences. But this — as Raisa Gorbacheva hinted in the synopsis of her thesis — was a paper formula which was not applied in practice. The everyday living conditions of collective farmers had hardly ever been investigated in detail.

Yet the concept of "daily life" (*byt*) had once been real enough, until it became a victim of Stalin's ruthless industrialization and indoctrination. Anatoli Lunacharsky, Soviet People's Commissar for Education and Culture between 1917 and 1929, wrote: "The real aim of the Revolution is the total transformation of the lifestyle: to give a cheerful and meaningful content to what is called private life." In 1926 he wrote: "Our young people are right when they try to be healthy, beautiful and even elegant."

Raisa Gorbacheva was one of the first who took up this thread again after 40 years. She was, in effect, a pioneer in sociology, a field hardly recognized in the Soviet Union. That is why Raisa Gorbacheva is called a "philosopher" and not a sociologist. Not until 1960 was a Department of Sociology created in the Philosophical Institute of the Academy of Sciences. A few years later — when sociology or social psychology "laboratories" had been set up at other universities and institutes (including Moscow, Leningrad, Novosibirsk, Sverdlovsk and Perm) — the Department of Sociology in the Philosophical Institute was enlarged. Not until 1968 was an independent Institute set up within the Academy for actual social research. One of its two Deputy Directors was Raisa Gorbacheva's doctoral supervisor, Osipov. Only in the late 1960's did investigations of Soviet everyday life begin to appear.

Yet among the scholars, who were scarcely qualified as sociologists, there was no agreement on the nature or the

political and ideological limits of this new branch of research. Techniques such as the methods of quantitative
social research were largely unknown. They were even
opposed whenever their first application produced undesir-
able results. The most striking aspect of this sociological
"pioneering" period was that the majority of the early
investigations came from towns and regions far from Moscow. This trend was due to the support of regional Party
Committees, like the one in Stavropol. To back their
ideological work, the committees needed analytical information on the social problems of the working class.

Here we have three important clues that help explain
Gorbachev's subsequent career and attitudes:

— Gorbachev, trained as a lawyer and agricultural economist, was influenced by his wife's sociological inquiries; her practical researches complemented his
  own view of Party work.
— in Stavropol, Gorbachev found the courage and the
  experience to place regional realism above bureaucratic centralism — which is why he has now furnished
  his power-base predominantly with regional Party
  Secretaries and experts — such as Yegor Ligachev,
  Nikolai Ryzhkov and Boris Yeltsin — rather than
  with old hands from Moscow headquarters.
— ever since the man from Stavropol transferred to Moscow in 1978, he has allowed more and more scope and
  influence to economists, sociologists and researchers
  into communal economics — such as Abel Aganbegyan, Tatyana Zaslavskaya, and Pyotr Bunich — and
  to regional institutes (Novosibirsk). These specialists
  are among his advisers today.

The involvement of such an unconventional couple as
Raisa and Mikhail Gorbachev would hardly have been
possible if the Stavropol Region had been controlled by a
narrowminded bureaucrat. It wasn't. The Party chief from
1960 onward was Fedor Davidovich Kulakov, who, like
Gorbachev, was the son of peasants and a supporter of
cautious experiments to modernize agriculture. In spite of

his "youth" — he was in his mid-forties — Kulakov was already one of Khrushchev's leading agricultural experts. A handsome man, looking more like a cultural official from Moscow than a provincial secretary, Kulakov thought highly of Gorbachev. In December 1962 he appointed him Head of the Party Organizations Department in the Stavropol Region Party Committee. This was a signal from Kulakov that Gorbachev might sooner or later succeed him, because this post controlled all the Party cadres throughout the Region.

In 1964 Kulakov was called to Moscow, where he was soon appointed as Central Committee Secretary for Agriculture, thus becoming supreme administrator of Soviet agriculture.

Kulakov's appointment showed Gorbachev that the important grain-growing region of Stavropol could be a vital springboard. Thereafter, even after becoming the Regional Party chief, he concentrated all his efforts on agriculture.

In September 1966 Gorbachev became First Secretary of the City of Stavropol. In this post he once more encountered Zdenek Mlynar. His fellow-student from the Lomonosov State University had since become a leading reform politician in Prague and, being on an official visit to Moscow, decided to visit Stavropol for a few days. The two of them talked about Khrushchev's fall and about the possibilities of introducing reforms in socialist countries. Gorbachev displayed no regrets about Khrushchev. Khrushchev, he believed, had essentially kept to the old method of arbitrary interference from the centre. His efforts at "decentralization" had been more in the nature of authoritarian intervention over the heads of those below him. He had indulged in campaigns and decrees, as if that were the only way to act. From Brezhnev, Gorbachev said, he expected a greater measure of autonomy and responsibility to be given to local leaders. According to Mlynar, Gorbachev considered decentralization essential for effective reforms in the economy and in politics.

In August 1968, when Soviet troops entered Czechoslovakia and the Central Committee Secretary Mlynar was temporarily taken to Moscow along with other top politicians of the Prague Spring, Gorbachev was still in Stavropol. As a result of Kulakov's support, he had just become Second Party Secretary. Then in April 1970, he became First Secretary.

How then did the new Party chief rule? He stirred up the region, but he did not set himself up as a pompous provincial boss. Like his predecessor, he lived in a single-storey house, a house painted green and dating from tsarist days, situated amidst the trees of Dzerzhinsky Street off Karl Marx Boulevard, opposite the local KGB headquarters. Gorbachev did not hide in his official black car or in the Party and administration building in Lenin Square. He usually walked the few hundred yards from his house to his office. Altogether he was more active, turning up more frequently to make inspections, than some officials would have liked. Because he kept pushing them, because he personally checked on the implementation of resolutions, because he held local officials responsible for their activities, he had a reputation for severity.

Even so, not everything in the region was as it should have been. A major problem was alcoholism. The fight against alcoholism, which Gorbachev is now waging throughout the Soviet Union, may have had its roots in this period. Towards the end of the 1970's, at about the time Gorbachev went to Moscow, *Literaturnaya Gazeta* reported from Stavropol: "It was an ordinary Monday, and no wages were being paid in any of Stavropol's enterprises. But there were lots of drunks.... At 7 p.m. began the battle for the staff of the Narcological Institute.... The drunks came in like an ocean wave. At midnight, when they were lying on their beds in a dead-drunk stupor, the Samaritans filled in the forms which informed the enterprises that their employees had been picked up in a state of drunkenness."

But in general Gorbachev ensured that his region made substantial progress. Under his leadership, work on the great Stavropol Canal proceeded at considerable speed. During his term as provincial Party chief, Gorbachev devoted himself to agriculture, and in doing so revealed three qualities that are at the core of his character: he was a courageous experimenter; he was quick to detect opposition and recognize the limits of his power; and he proved enough of a tactician to retain his objectives without impairing his prospects.

In the early 1970's he introduced in his fertile province a bonus system based on results, without the customary controls or quotas. Work teams, which might be formed by groups of peasants or by families on the basis of contracts, were paid according to the results of their harvest and according to their expenses. By the mid-1970's, nearly 1,500 such mechanized brigades were operating without prescribed quotas in the Stavropol Region. In 1976 the Stavropol Party decided to apply the system across the board in the Region. According to newspaper reports of the day, so *Ekonomicheskaya Gazeta* reports, harvest yields achieved by quota-free brigades were up by 50 percent on irrigated land, and by 30–40 percent on non-irrigated land.

But suddenly, in the following year, Gorbachev introduced an even newer and allegedly even more progressive form of organization for agriculture: the so-called Ipatovo method, named after the district in the Stavropol Region where it was first applied. It represented a complete reversal of the brigade system, which it had been hoped would stimulate the peasants' personal interest. The Ipatovo method was a return to the "grand style": mobile fleets of harvesters and transporters were employed, not on individual farms but for the entire area. The exceptionally good harvest results in the Stavropol Region in 1977, for which the quota-free brigade system had created the prerequisites, were attributed solely to the Ipatovo method. The Central Committee in Moscow gave its blessing to this "new" pattern. General Secretary Leonid Brezhnev congratulated the Ipatovo District on its great achievement.

However, the enthusiasm was short-lived. The big fleets brought new problems with them. Years later, after Gorbachev had become a powerful man in Moscow, *Izvestiya* (September 29 1983) published a shattering balance sheet:

"All those fleets of machinery set up by the Ipatovo method! But if you look closely — nothing. They simply do not exist. Moreover, the situation has in fact got worse than before. All the machines are concentrated in large units, often quite unnecessarily. And then a whole armada of farm machinery rolls off in one direction or another because conditions are right for harvesting a few fields — but two combine harvesters would be enough. And on the other hand there are fields which cannot be harvested until the fleets of machinery have completed their tasks elsewhere." In the same year, and again reported in *Izvestiya*, Gorbachev once more recommended the quota-free brigades: "As a rule they glean 20 to 30 percent more from their patch of land, with less effort and at lower cost. Moreover, their earnings are of course higher. Over the past few years the number of quota-free brigades has increased.... However, this progressive method is still not being extended fast enough."

What induced Gorbachev to make the about-turn to the Ipatovo method in the first place? Why did he abandon the quota-free brigade system in 1977, only to embrace it again in 1983? Clearly the provincial Party chief's enthusiasm for reform ran into opposition in Moscow. In this situation, which was not entirely free from risks, Gorbachev preferred to play the flexible, adaptable pragmatist. In retrospect it seems as if he wanted to dispel the suspicions of his more powerful opponents by switching over as rapidly as possible to the Ipatovo method; but far from revising his own ideas, he merely put them on ice to await a more favourable moment.

This came sooner than expected. In July 1978 Gorbachev's patron Fedor Kulakov died. It came as a shock. Kulakov had radiated youthful optimism. He had also been in line for even higher office. He had been a Central Committee Secretary since 1965 and in April 1971 he had in addition become a Member of the Politburo. With the combination of these two top posts, he had become one of the circle of potential "crown princes," and the first candidate of the next generation among the geriatric Kremlin leadership. According to the official version he died of a coronary. But it is now known that he committed suicide; he was found with his wrists cut. There has never been any reliable information about his motives, but at the time of his death rumour had it that he had been at the centre of a furious argument in the Party. The funeral ceremony in Red Square, on July 19 1978, certainly had some unusual features. General Secretary Brezhnev, Premier Kosygin, the chief ideologist Suslov, and Brezhnev's intimate Chernenko all failed to attend. The funeral commission, on the other hand, included one man, a plain Central Committee member, who had until then escaped the attention of foreign observers in Moscow. The man, who had, it was noticed, a red birthmark on his head, gave one of the funeral orations. It was Mikhail Gorbachev's first Red Square speech.

Four months later, in November 1978, he again turned up in Moscow. Gorbachev had succeeded Fedor Kulakov as Central Committee Secretary for Agriculture. This time the Kremlin watchers made a rapid and somewhat surprised mental note of his face. An unknown 47-year-old from the provinces had suddenly entered the circle of the geriatric leadership. Fourteen years below the average age of the Politburo, he seemed to be the vanguard of an up-and-coming generation.

Who had called Gorbachev to Moscow? The names of two Politburo Members are always mentioned — Mikhail Suslov and Yuri Andropov.

That Mikhail Suslov, the rigid custodian of ideological dogma, should have smoothed the road for the unorthodox experimenter from Stavropol seems at first glance rather unlikely. Admittedly Suslov had once been the Party chief of the Stavropol Region — but that was nearly 40 years before Gorbachev was called to Moscow. A possible explanation of Suslov's sympathy might instead be found in his specific personal philosophy. The chief ideologist, who died in 1982, was a nationalist and — compared with Brezhnev's clique — positively ascetic. Nothing was more important to him than the Russian land. The young, well-educated yet earthy Russian from Stavropol, whose region was not drowning in corruption and incompetence but was directing all its efforts to agriculture, may have appeared to Suslov as a counterweight to Brezhnev's clique.

There can be no doubt that even before his brief time as General Secretary, Andropov was one of Gorbachev's patrons. For a number of years the two had shared the same ideas about the urgent need for modernization. This feeling had been strengthened by meetings in the Caucasian mineral spas, where Andropov, suffering from kidney disease, frequently took the waters and where Gorbachev as the Regional Party chief had to welcome distinguished visitors from Moscow. It is a favourite story in Moscow that the intellectual and highly educated KGB chief was also impressed by Raisa Gorbacheva. What is certain is that Andropov, always a single-minded worker, suffered a collapse at the spa of Kislovodsk long before the West knew anything about his illness. It seems very likely, therefore, that in the prolonged and thorough preparations for his own accession, Andropov included Gorbachev in his plans as his principal organizer and as his "crown prince."

If Gorbachev had been a Party chief in Murmansk, up in the north, he would almost certainly not have attained the post of General Secretary. He would never have had the contacts to which Stavropol gave him access. But in addition to contacts, the man from Stavropol also had some impressive achievements behind him. And his integrity, drive and managerial skills were beyond reproach.

Andropov, who with all his hardness as KGB chief also had a lyrical and sentimental side to him (as was shown after his death when some of his poems were reproduced in a documentary on his life), had another reason for favouring his affable host. The road which Gorbachev had to take from Stavropol each time he called on the Moscow VIPs at the mineral spas, a road climbing through the ravined foothills, also ran past a small derelict railway station with a few scattered houses. The name of that station is Naguts-kaya. It would not be worth a mention were it not the spot where Andropov was born. Andropov might well have been proud of having found in his own region a man whom he could trust to lead the Soviet Union into the 21st century.

4

The War Against
the Veterans

In the 23 years since Gorbachev left Moscow, much had changed.

When Josef Stalin died, on March 5 1953, his entourage instantly realized that the country could no longer be ruled in his way. Within a few days of his death, a mass amnesty was declared. Three months later, the chief of Stalin's secret police, Beria, was arrested. Cautious relaxations followed over the next two years. Finally, at the 20th Party Congress in 1956, Nikita Khrushchev made his sensational revelations of Stalin's crimes in the hope of banning the despot's shadow forever.

Khrushchev's motives were anything but philanthropical. He wished to separate himself from the oligarchs squabbling about Stalin's inheritance, and set himself up as the genius of a new golden age. He was playing for high stakes. And in the end he lost. He made the bureaucrats nervous. He backed consumerism and missiles, neglecting other weapons and the Armed Forces, and thereby undermined his own position. After eight years, he finally succumbed to his opponents.

The next leader, Leonid Brezhnev, rigidly applied the lessons learned from Khrushchev's fall. He avoided any semblance of erratic behaviour, and he once more covered up Stalin's crimes in order to hide the Party's failure. Brezhnev did not court the "confidence of the masses" as a way of controlling the Party elite, the way Khrushchev had done. He endeavoured to re-establish a closed society by opting for "confidence in the Party cadres." In doing so, he gave the bureaucrats — who under Stalin had been in perpetual fear of their lives and under Khrushchev in fear of their posts — a sense of peace, community and stability. Yet they used peace only for personal benefits; their communal links served corruption; and their stability became stagnation.

Initially, however, events proved Brezhnev right. When Stalin died, a collective farmer earned just 24 kopeks a day — 6 roubles per month — and could afford one pair of trousers each year. In 1978 he was earning about 100 roubles a month. (By 1985 the figure had risen to some 140 roubles a month.) This was little enough, but it has to be seen against the history of a country where wages prior to the Revolution had been below subsistence level and where in the early 1930's a large number of peasants had actually died of starvation. The first decade under Brezhnev (1965–1975) was, in economic and social terms, domestically and internationally the most successful decade in Soviet history. The growth rate was nearly six percent annually. Leadership cadres and factions within the Party were more willing to compromise. Abroad, the Soviet Union was acknowledged by President Nixon to be a world power ranking equal with the United States.

After the mid-1970's, however, the pace slackened. Power production slowed. Agriculture lagged further and further behind, despite the investment of vast sums. In certain industries and occupations a shortage of manpower began to emerge. The Army had to recruit an ever greater number of young men from the less industrialized areas of Central Asia. Industry could not do the same, for the Muslim peoples of the Soviet Union are not willing to migrate.

These trends seemed particularly alarming as the industrialized west of the Soviet Union was beginning to show a marked decline in birth rate. Given the nature of city life

— urbanization without urban culture, low-quality food, poor accommodation, alcoholism, divorce — the trend seemed irreversible. In addition, Moscow's attempts to offset the technological lead of American arms production siphoned off increasing numbers from the manufacture of consumer goods for the domestic market. Supplies to the public dwindled.

Soviet citizens reacted to all this in the same "counter-revolutionary" manner as the Poles did in August 1980, except that they did so within the framework of their own traditions. The Poles refused to work as a nation; in the Soviet Union, the same recalcitrance had long been prac-tised by millions as individuals. They "struck" against their low wages and shortages by doing their shopping during working hours and by loafing about when they should have been working.

The reaction of many Soviet citizens to the obvious short-comings of the system was curiously ambivalent. Just as if Stalin's victims had never existed, a naive belief sprang up that the great dictator would have solved all economic problems. And the deeper Brezhnev's regime sank into lethargy and corrupt self-interest, the more Soviet citizens, chatting in queues, in beer parlours and at bus stops, praised the dead Generalissimo. Stalin had reduced prices every year, they said, and made sure of proper discipline. During the discussion of the new Constitution in 1977, *Pravda* was said to have received 40,000 letters from read-ers calling for greater discipline.

But what was much more relevant politically was the country's fundamental mood. As the competence of the Soviet leadership declined, and as large sections of the population began to display a mild hankering after disci-pline, the rising elites demanded rejuvenation at the top, not just metaphorically, but physically as well. New men, and younger ones.

Yuri Andropov, for many years the KGB chief, perceived this mood more clearly than anyone else. To suit it, he devised a dual strategy — first, to win power through a campaign against corruption and, next, to tighten up the

Soviet system and make it more efficient.

Andropov, then the shrewdest and coolest head in the Politburo, had long been blocked by Brezhnev's clique. As recently as the 26th Party Congress he had neither presented a report nor chaired a session. In the hierarchy of the Politburo, he ranked only eighth — at least that was his place when the Politburo appeared in full strength. He did not possess any power-base of his own in the struggle against Brezhnev's clique. True, the state security apparatus was his tool, but he could not apply it publicly to mobilize the younger generation against the gerontocracy, the experts against the bureaucrats, or the managers against the ministries.

Instead, to get his way, he allowed ever greater scope to criticism from scientific institutions and in the media, deliberately loosening the KGB's reins. In this way, he increased the pressure of the outside world against the internal world, that of the academics against the apparatus, that of the elites against the officials.

Yet these newly arrayed forces on the outside needed their own champions at the centre of power, top candidates inside the Kremlin, disciplined younger men representative of the next generation.

This was the role which Gorbachev assumed in Moscow, in closely orchestrated collusion with Andropov. Rising more rapidly than anyone since Stalin's death, the new Central Committee Secretary for Agriculture moved into the centre of power (interestingly, Gorbachev had never managed the Central Committee Department for Agriculture, which suggests that Andropov had earmarked him for different tasks from the very start). In 1979 he became a Candidate Member of the Politburo. Only a year later, six months before his 50th birthday, he moved into the Politburo as a full Member. Politburo Member plus Central Committee Secretary — a dual function that signalled his membership of the innermost circle of leadership.

Anyone combining these offices must play one of three roles: a rival to the Party chief, or an elderly "king-maker," or a "crown prince." When Gorbachev moved into that

circle only four others held those two functions: Leonid
Brezhnev by virtue of his office of General Secretary;
Mikhail Suslov, the "king-maker"; Andrei Kirilenko, an
earlier "crown prince" but now in decline; and Konstantin
Chernenko, the man favoured by Brezhnev to succeed him.

All these men belonged to a different generation. When
Stalin died, the average age of the Politburo Members was
55.4, that of Politburo Candidate Members 50.9 and that of
Central Committee Secretaries 52. When Brezhnev
assumed power the averages had already gone up: to 61,
52.8, and 54.1 respectively. When Gorbachev, not quite 50,
moved into the Politburo in 1980, the leaders were all, on
average, pensionable: the average for Politburo Members
was 70.1, for Candidate Members 62.5, and for Central
Committee Secretaries 67.

The aging Party leaders had become alienated not only
from the masses but also from the rising top people in
institutions, enterprises and provincial governments. Gorbachev soon established links with these groups, collected
information, commissioned expert opinions, and cautiously
introduced certain nuances into his speeches to accommodate their common interests. Gorbachev and the young
elite outside the Kremlin found common ground in refus-
ing to pursue foreign interests as a substitute for domestic
change — a policy that distinguished them from most of
the pre-Revolutionary reformers.

Yuri Andropov, who could not become a candidate for the
succession in the normal way, simply because the post of
KGB chief did not look good in a "crown prince," pushed his
way up to the top from behind with Gorbachev at his side.
This manoeuvre he performed in two phases.

First, he left Chernenko a free hand in his duel with the
long-term "crown prince" Kirilenko. Since both Andropov
and Gorbachev were to profit considerably from Kirilenko's legacy, his role was of some significance. A qualified engineer and the Central Committee Secretary responsible for industry, Kirilenko was a man who would
make a hard leader. Yet he supported limited economic
reform within the framework of a central planning system,

including financial incentives for industry. In the mid-1970's, at the peak of his power, he brought to Moscow Yakov Ryabov, a man from his own industrial and political power-base of Sverdlovsk in the Urals, whom he made Central Committee Secretary. Soon, however, Ryabov lost his post and in 1979 was shunted off into the State Planning Commission. This signalled Kirilenko's diminishing power.

As the scales tipped in favour of Brezhnev's preferred candidate, Chernenko, Andropov suddenly opened up a second front against him with his anti-corruption campaign. Andropov gradually won over Kirilenko's supporters, and eventually emerged triumphant from the power struggle. The opening of Andropov's campaign, in which he had Gorbachev on his side, caused the greatest confusion in Moscow since Khrushchev's time. From the end of 1981, Leonid Brezhnev suddenly became the object of scurrilous attacks. The first rounds against the sick Party chief, who by then was scarcely capable of work, were fired by the Leningrad Writers' Union's monthly journal, which bore the glorious name of *Aurora*, the cruiser whose salvoes inaugurated the October Revolution. The periodical devoted its December issue to the Party chief's 75th birthday. It was a backhanded compliment. On page 75 — the page number making the reference perfectly obvious — a caricature of a supposedly fictitious poet-cum-superman bore the unmistakable features of Brezhnev. Portraying him as a poet was an allusion to the fact that a few months earlier he had allowed himself to be awarded the Lenin Prize for Literature for his turgid memoirs. The satirical text said, among other things: "Most people think of him as if he had long been dead, so great is the veneration of his talent.... It is difficult to believe that he will have to die one day. And he himself probably does not believe that he will die." At the conclusion of the article, its author, Viktor Golyadkin, expressed the confident hope that "we shall not have long to wait before we hear the praises which will be showered upon that author upon his death. We all believe in him. Let us hope that he will complete the work he still has in hand

and make our hearts rejoice as soon as possible."

This scarcely concealed piece of malice could never have passed the very strict censorship of the tough Leningrad Party chief Grigori Romanov unless it was carefully planned at the highest level. (Romanov was subsequently brought to Moscow, to the centre of power, by the victorious Andropov and made a Central Committee secretary.)

Shortly after *Aurora's* salvo, Soviet sources in Moscow began to draw the attention of foreigners to the fact that the Party chief was now nothing but the helpless tool of his corrupt clan of relations. They reported that the authorities were investigating the long-standing lover of Brezhnev's 53-year-old daughter Galina. The man, a shadowy figure known as Boris the Gipsy, was a playboy and bit-part actor at the Bolshoi Theatre. The police were said to have found diamonds of the tsarist era in his possession. These jewels, according to this explosive gossip, had been stolen from the flat of a lady lion-tamer who worked at the Moscow State Circus. The director of this world-famous circus, Anatoli Kolevatov, was also implicated. As one of the circle around Brezhnev's daughter, he had enabled artists to travel abroad on condition that they brought back for him luxury goods for the Moscow black market. In an interview with *Pravda*, the popular clown Yuri Nikulin indirectly tried to turn public opinion against Kolevatov. His interviewer was an until then anonymous woman reporter, Galina Kozhukhova. Her first name was significant: it hinted at the real target of the attack, Brezhnev's daughter Galina. On February 22 1982, *Pravda* (whose editor-in-chief Viktor Afanasyev had supported Andropov from the start, and subsequently supported Gorbachev) published a commentary on readers' letters about private morals. In it, *Pravda* quoted a sentence from one of those letters: "Children reveal, as if in a mirror, the psychological conditions and convictions which prevail in their families."

These attacks on the sick Party chief and his clique had a secondary target: Konstantin Chernenko, Brezhnev's preferred candidate. The implied message was: How can a

helpless old man, who can no longer control his own corrupt family, choose the right successor?

A key role in the affair of Brezhnev's family was played
by his vain brother-in-law, General Semyon Tsvigun, First
Deputy Chairman of the KGB. But as for the precise part
played by the general, accounts differed.

According to one imaginative version, Tsvigun insisted
that Boris the Gipsy, the diamond-loving friend of Brezhnev's daughter, had to be arrested. Tsvigun was even reported to have threatened to lay criminal charges against
Brezhnev's alcoholic son Yuri, a Deputy Minister of Foreign Trade. Faced with this unparalleled KGB attack on the
sanctity of the Soviet Party chief, seeking to avoid a Kremlin Watergate, Suslov, the ascetic custodian of the Revolution, summoned and questioned Tsvigun.

Today, however, it is clear from more reliable sources
that Tsvigun himself covered up the doings of Brezhnev's
daughter in order to protect her and her friends from investigation. Andropov was said to have passed on the files on
Galina's criminal friends to Suslov at the beginning of
1982. Suslov, personally above any suspicion of corruptibil-
ity, had been so alarmed at the extent of the Brezhnev's
clique's economic offences that in mid-January he chal-
lenged Tsvigun to make a statement. The clash between
the Party's No. 2 and the KGB's No. 2 — on this point the
different versions again converged — was so serious that
Suslov had, in the end, threatened the general with expulsion from the Party, among other dire fates.

On January 19 1982 Tsvigun died. Officially, he had had
"a serious and prolonged illness." Simultaneously, however, rumour had it that the KGB general had committed
suicide. Two days later Suslov had a coronary; on January
25 his heart finally failed. The official cause: arterioscler-
osis and diabetes. Unofficial Moscow sources reported that
the clashes with Tsvigun had been the final straw for the
frail Suslov.

Tsvigun — First Deputy Chairman of the KGB, a general and a member of the Central Committee — was not
given the grave of honour appropriate to his rank in the

VIP cemetery at the Novodevichy Monastery. The communique about his death, contrary to custom, lacked the
signatures of his brother-in-law Brezhnev and of most
Politburo Members. Only four men from the Party's top
body signed it: Chernenko, Ustinov, Andropov and Gorbachev, a confirmation that Gorbachev had been active in
support of Andropov in the disputes between the KGB and
Brezhnev's clique.

Immediately after Suslov's death, Andropov and his sup-
porters continued their campaign against corruption. On
January 26, the day following Suslov's death, when the
Party leadership was busy with the preparations for his
funeral, Boris the Gipsy was arrested. Shortly afterwards
the investigators also ordered the arrest of circus director
Kolevatov, even though he held the rank of a Deputy
Minister of Culture, on charges of serious currency off-
ences. Two and a half years later, in September 1984,
Kolevatov was sentenced to 13 years' imprisonment.

On January 29 1982 Mikhail Suslov was buried by the
Kremlin Wall. According to custom, he lay in state in an
open coffin. Brezhnev, now scarcely able to take in what
was going on around him and mercilessly exposed on television, called out in a frail voice: "Sleep in peace, dear
friend!"

His enemies lost no time in making sure Suslov's policies
were well and truly buried with him. Andropov opened a
new offensive on the issue of ideology, thus giving notice of
his claim to the role of chief ideologist and the No. 2 post in
the Party. On February 1 *Pravda*, out of the blue, attacked
the nationalist wing of the Moscow intelligentsia. This
loosely knit group of russophiles have no name for themselves, but they are known in Germany as "Russites," by
analogy with "Hussites," the 15th-century Czech nationalists who followed Jan Huss.

Russite nationalism has a bizarre rationale. They are
the heirs of the Pan-Slavs and Slavophiles of the late 19th
century, who asserted the superiority of Russian values
over Teutonic and Roman influences. To them, Lenin is
suspect. For him, the extension of the Russian empire was

a means to achieve world revolution, not an end in itself. It was Stalin who re-asserted Russian hegemony, transforming the Comintern (the Communist International) into an instrument for the expansion of Russia. For this reason, Russites see Stalin as a true expression of Russian history, and his purges as the cleansing of the homeland from Western, Marxist and Jewish subversion.

The Russites, the latter-day Pan-Slavs, find considerable support in the Moscow Institute of Mathematics, the political administration of the Army, the Young Guard publishing house, and the Ministry of Culture. Russite tendencies even have supporters in the cultural section of the Central Committee. For many years Suslov had been their covert supporter.

Now *Pravda* served notice that Russite extremism — and thus Suslov's ideas — were not acceptable. The half-page *Pravda* article bore the innocuous headline "Precision of Criteria — A Survey of Literature." It contained a sharp attack by a professor of literature, V. Kuleshov, on Vadim Kozhinov of the Moscow Institute of World Literature, a ruthless champion of anti-Semitic and chauvinist thinking. Kuleshov mercilessly criticized Kozhinov for "distorting the truth." His opinions, expressed in one of his articles, had robbed "Russian literature of its deeply rooted fundamental characteristic of commitment to social criticism and civil enlightenment." Kozhinov, ran the *Pravda* piece, was "defiling" the patriotic significance of the Battle of Kulikovo (at which, in 1380, the Grand Duke of Muscovy defeated a superior Tartar army).

The real purpose of this attack from behind the cloak of literary criticism was more clearly revealed a few days later. On February 13, *Pravda* published a fundamental declaration on the political position of the Italian Communist Party. The article represented a surprising ideological U-turn. Only three weeks before, when Suslov was still alive, the official Party newspaper had condemned the Italian Communist Party in terms reminiscent of Tito's "excommunication" (which had also been signed by Suslov) in 1948. *Pravda* had reprimanded Berlinguer for criticizing the state of emergency proclaimed in Poland by General Jaruzelski: "In today's world this amounts to direct assistance to imperialism," it said. The decisions of the Italian Party leaders were "a heavy blow to the struggle for peace." Yet now the Soviet Party's official newspaper expressly praised "the contribution of the Italian communists to the struggle for detente."

This was the first clear signal from those in the Kremlin who were about to loosen the chains of Suslov's dogmatism. It was not Brezhnev's death, nine months later, that marked the turning point. It was the departure of Suslov. Now that the Kremlin's wall was breached, Andropov immediately seized his advantage, and the young guard around Gorbachev were allowed to present to the country some economic facts and figures as a change from the traditional salvoes of ideology.

It would be facile to portray the "young reformer" Gorbachev as the opponent of the "old dogmatist" Suslov. But if ever there was a politician who, while pursuing the same objective of making the Soviet Union the most powerful state on earth, differed from Gorbachev not just in age, but in bearing and style, in strategy and tactics, in language and perception of the world, then that man was Mikhail Suslov.

He was the pope of counter-reformation in communism and he held his ideological custodianship for more than 35 years. His faith in Soviet dogma was rooted in the period immediately following the October Revolution. The son of peasants, he was accepted as an economist into the Institute of Red Professors — just when Stalin was taking power out of Lenin's hands. Using Stalin's so-called "iron broom," the young Party official cleared the road for his own political career. In 1939 Suslov became Party chief in Stavropol, the native region of the then eight-year-old Gorbachev. In 1944 — after organizing the deportation of the anti-Soviet, pro-German Karachai tribe — he became Chairman of the Politburo in conquered Lithuania. There he entrenched Soviet rule against bitter partisan resistance. In 1952, at the 19th Party Congress — when the Moscow student Gorbachev joined the Soviet Communist Party — Suslov moved up into the Politburo. At the end of Brezhnev's regime he was the only one left in the Politburo who had been a full Member of this top-level body since Stalin's reign.

After Stalin's death, the lanky, short-sighted professor with the distinctive tousled hair became the champion of collective leadership in the Kremlin. Even though he was an unrepentant disciple of Stalin's centralism, he evidently realized that there must never again be unlimited one-man dictatorship in the Kremlin. Because he rejected the personality cult and the concentration of power in one pair of hands, he condemned Stalin posthumously. But he equally rejected Khrushchev's de-Stalinization and reforming zeal, especially as he saw it as yet another one-man performance. Khrushchev's rapprochement with the West after his meeting with Eisenhower at Camp David, his plan for the demobilization of 1.2 million troops, his acceptance of West Germany — all these individualistic decisions met with opposition on the part of Suslov, who had by then become the Kremlin's Grey Eminence. When Khrushchev, in his impulsive way, began to try to dismantle the collective leadership, Suslov initiated a palace revolt against him. On October 13 1964, Suslov had Khrushchev brought back from holiday by the future Defence Minister Ustinov. In front of the Presidium and Central Committee he dispassionately listed Khrushchev's sins. Khrushchev, flushed with anger, clenched his fists and shouted insults. Thereupon Suslov rose to his feet again and commented coolly: "You can see for yourselves, comrades — there's little point in working with him any more!"

Under Brezhnev, whom Suslov the king-maker had himself chosen for the succession, he remained the Party's No. 2 right to the end. He never gave up his self-elected role of watchdog. In July 1970 he prevented Brezhnev from combining the offices of chief of Party and head of government. Brezhnev's policy of detente, which was originally designed for long-term co-operation and which presumed permanent stability of the Western partner and of the international situation, was opposed by Suslov with his demands for world revolution. For years, through the dogma of the Kremlin's infallibility, he tried to stem the currents of communist reform throughout the world.

Suslov torpedoed the policy of detente. He intervened whenever fraternal Parties attempted reform. He rushed to Budapest immediately before the crushing of the Hungarian Rising in 1956. In the Prague Spring of 1968, he subjected Dubcek's leadership to cross-examination. And in 1981, at the height of the Polish Solidarity movement, he was in Warsaw. Yet this great-Russian zealot of revolutionary dogma was no political adventurer, no mailed-fist communist. Right to the end he voted against military intervention in Budapest and Prague. Regarded by orthodox Communist Party bureaucrats throughout Europe as their pope, Suslov was worried that Moscow's role in the world communist movement might be compromised.

What then did Suslov believe in? When Stalin's daughter Svetlana once applied for her passport to India, Suslov was astonished: "What on earth tempts you to go abroad? Why have my family and myself never felt any wish to go there? Surely it is of no interest whatever!" Suslov's philosophy was quite simple: Russia was the centre of the universe.

After February 1982, Andropov, Gorbachev and the men of the younger generation, who regarded the traditional view as no longer tenable because it was based only on Suslov's theories and not on results, began to develop and to apply new criteria. At the end of May, after 15 years in office as KGB chief, Andropov relinquished this post because it was now not only an impediment to his struggle for Brezhnev's succession but was damaging to his reputation abroad. Succeeding Suslov, he became Central Committee Secretary for Ideology, International Party Relations and Foreign Policy. It was a preliminary step in the power struggle against Konstantin Chernenko.

Andropov used the summer to tighten his grip on the Brezhnev clique with his anti-corruption campaign, starting a purge not only of Brezhnev's family circle but also of his Party friends. In July 1982 the First Secretary of the Krasnodar Region in southern Russia, Sergei Medunov, was relieved of his post. Medunov had not only looked after Brezhnev's *dacha* near Sochi, but as the Party chief of the Krasnodar Region had been responsible for the *dachas* of the Moscow VIPs along this famous stretch of Black Sea coast. To clean up Krasnodar, Andropov brought in Vitali Vorotnikov, a man who, as one of Kirilenko's "private guard," had been shunted off to Cuba as ambassador in 1979. Vorotnikov soon became a key figure — purging rather than reforming — in the new drive for order and discipline; he rose to the Politburo and was one of Gorbachev's closer allies.

Brezhnev's son-in-law, Galina's husband Yuri Churbanov, a lieutenant-general and Deputy Minister of the Interior, was likewise pushed out. In November 1981, on the Day of the Militia, Churbanov had stated in *Izvestiya*: "State and people demand that the Militia's actions should be maximally efficient, so that every crime is duly solved and the culprits appropriately punished." Andropov's investigators took him at his word, and sent him to Murmansk. In February 1985 a spokesman for the Ministry of the Interior announced that he had been relieved of his post.

On November 9 1982, one day before Brezhnev's death, the manager of the most famous and oldest-established Moscow food store, Gastronom No. 1, Yuri Sokolov, was detained. He and his wife, who had been in charge of a special section of the GUM department store and was now arrested along with him, had been friendly with Galina. On November 25 1983 Sokolov was sentenced to death for crimes against the economy. On July 14 1984 the Moscow evening paper *Vechernyaya Moskva* carried a brief item to the effect that Sokolov's petition for clemency had been turned down and the sentence executed.

Brezhnev himself was spared even more embarrassing

revelations, such as the dismissal, soon afterwards, of his friend and Minister of the Interior Nikolai Shcholokov for corruption within his sphere of office. At 11 a.m. on November 11 1982 Soviet television's chief newsreader, Igor Kirilov, with tears in his eyes, announced that "Leonid Ilyich Brezhnev, General Secretary of the CPSU Central Committee and Chairman of the USSR Supreme Soviet Presidium, died suddenly on November 10 at 8.30 hours."

The following day, the Central Committee elected 68-year-old Andropov to be his successor.

5
Andropov's Year of Transition

On his accession to power, Yuri Andropov allowed himself to be portrayed Janus-faced: to the West he showed reformist, almost bourgeois, features, while to his own people he displayed the mien of a stern ruler.

Reputable Western publications seized upon the urbane, Western image he presented to them. The *Wall Street Journal* reported on Andropov's liking for "Glenn Miller records, good scotch whisky, Oriental rugs, and American books." *Time* described him as a "bibliophile" and "connoisseur of modern art" dressed in clothes "sharply tailored in a West European style." As a "perfect host," according to the *Washington Post*, he would invite "leading dissidents to his home for well-lubricated discussions that sometimes extended to the small hours." Indeed "a casual visitor to his country house" — according to the distinguished American journalist Harrison Salisbury — "found him listening to an English-language *Voice of America* broadcast." The last remnants of socialism to which Andropov still clung were, according to these accounts, Hungarian furniture, the gift of Janos Kadar.

Most of these details, which are largely mythical, come from a single source: from Vladimir Sakharov who defected in 1971 as a 26-year-old diplomat and can provide such colourful gossip because, according to his own account, he was a schoolmate of Andropov's son Igor. Sakharov's lurid tales were accepted unchecked by the American quality press.

There would be no point in harking back to this episode were it not for the fact that it reveals the existence, long before Gorbachev, of a secret longing on the part of many Western journalists and politicians for "a smart man in Moscow." Such hopes are quite natural: we have seen how they were nourished by Gorbachev's affable behaviour in London. But the fact that even the ex-KGB chief Andropov — who never (at least officially) visited a capitalist country — so readily found Western approval provides an explanation of the Gorbachev myth which has grown enormously since the end of 1984. Gorbachev won sympathy during his visits to Britain, Italy and Canada not solely because of his social graces, but because of a widespread antipathy to seeing the Soviet Union portrayed as an "empire of evil" and the Kremlin as exclusively peopled by immovable bureaucrats.

Andropov was not one of those bureaucrats. Stefan Zweig's portrayal of Joseph Fouché, the Jacobin revolutionary who became Napoleon's Minister of Police, would seem to fit Andropov well: "In spirit he belongs to the race of cold-blooded creatures. He has no gross overwhelming passions, he is not driven to women, nor to gambling either, he takes no wine, he takes no pleasure in extravagant spending, he does not flex his muscles, he only lives indoors among documents and papers.... The awareness of power as such suffices: he needs neither its badge nor its garment.... he is ambitious to the highest, to the very highest, degree but he is not hungry for glory; he is ambitious without being vain."

In some respects, of course, the two men were very different: by the standards of the French intriguer, Andropov was a paragon of probity and principle. Yet Zweig's words are a fairly good portrayal of his ascetic style of life and work. The members of Andropov's brief administration were relatively modest in their accumulation of wealth and power — and relatively firm against those who used that power to the advantage of themselves and their proteges.

The sixth Soviet leader after Lenin (1917–1924), Stalin (1924–1953), Malenkov (1953, only for a few days), Khrushchev (1953–1964) and Brezhnev (1964–1982), Andropov was on his accession older and more experienced than any of his predecessors. At 68, he had previously been KGB Chairman for 15 years. None of his 11 predecessors as Soviet security chiefs had managed such a leap up. But Andropov had also spent 27 years in the Party machine. No Party chief before him had been a professional foreign-policy man and none of his Politburo colleagues had directly experienced a popular rising, as Andropov had while ambassador in Hungary in 1956.

Andropov was the first Kremlin leader to inherit a superpower whose military might matched that of its rival. Thanks to his many years as KGB Chairman, he was also better informed than anyone else on how the multiple sicknesses of the Soviet economy impaired the empire's military strength. Though suffering from a kidney complaint even when he assumed office, he proceeded to spur his arthritic country into action. He realized, of course, that he could no longer reform society from the bottom up, so he devoted his dwindling strength to a reorganization from the top downwards.

Brezhnev had created a state of affairs that was unprecedented in Soviet history and probably also unrepeatable. He had based his leadership on the complacent harmony of the Party leaders. In that sense Andropov was not a Party man. He played down its ruling role in his speeches. He based his own short-lived rule on those three pillars of the state whose representatives Brezhnev had brought into the Politburo in 1973: the KGB, the Armed Forces, and the diplomatic service.

Andropov sought to weaken the Party leaders by separating them from these supports. He thus became the greatest challenger to the system since Khrushchev. He set out to fight his country's parasitical and stagnant bureaucracy using the instruments of the police state. He did not want to liberalize: he wanted to mobilize reserves. This meant structural change. To the rising elite this programme seemed promising. But to the old Kremlin leadership, it marked the end of a way of life, the end of bland camaraderie, the end of the "stability of the cadres."

The significance of Andropov's aims was missed by many Western observers because they were presented in controversial, sometimes arcane, statements of policy. At the first plenary meeting of the Central Committee after Brezhnev's death, on November 22 1982, the new General Secretary announced that "the independence of associations and enterprises, of collective and state farms, must be increased." "The solution to this question must be approached practically," Andropov declared. "Experiments must be carried out when necessary." Anxious to justify the intended corrections to the Soviet system in Marxist terminology, even though Chernenko, as the Party's No. 2, had formally taken on the role of chief ideologist, Andropov told the plenary meeting of the Central Committee in June 1983: "A historical point has been reached, when profound qualitative changes in the productive forces and production relations have not only become ripe but unavoidable."

Yet confusingly, in an article on the 100th anniversary of Marx's death in *Kommunist* (February 1983), he pleaded not for experiments but for law and order. "What comes foremost?" he wrote. "According to Marx's words, it is the consistent strengthening of law and order in all spheres of the national economy."

While Andropov was displaying the tough face of reform, Gorbachev did not formulate his appeals for greater discipline in quite such narrow terms. Charles de Gaulle once joked about France that a country with 360 types of cheese cannot be ruled dictatorially. How much harder then to dictate to a state with more than 100 national groups and 11 time zones! No, Gorbachev was considerably subtler in his thinking than his mentor, Andropov.

Shortly after the publication of Andropov's article, Gorbachev gave his views on how to achieve economic revival.

Significantly, he presented them at a festive meeting to mark the 113th anniversary of Lenin's birth, on April 22 1983. His remarks, with their indirect invocation of Lenin's NEP policy, are of exceptional importance for an understanding of Gorbachev's thinking. "Our reliable support, here as always, is Lenin's legacy, his teaching of democratic centralism," Gorbachev said. "Lenin persistently defended centralism as the *point of departure* [author's italics — it was not the once-and-for-all policy] in the organization of the economy of socialism, which represents a uniform entity. At the same time he called for a free rein to be given to creativity and initiative at the base: 'Our main task [Lenin said] is to provide an impetus everywhere in the country, to mobilize a maximum of initiative and to display a maximum of independence'." Gorbachev was thus pointing to structural changes to ensure a political and economic revival, rather than contenting himself with declarations about discipline pure and simple.

Though it was not at all obvious until later, what Gorbachev had actually fixed his aim on was not the central planning system as a whole, but the bureaucratic central structure. The overall targets should continue to be set from the centre. But the stifling control of the ministries and State apparatus, which killed initiative and responsibility amongst the workers, had to be trimmed back. This was to take place with the help of the media and expanded public discussion.

Optimum decisions by the authorities, he said, were "unthinkable without careful consideration of the collected experiences of scientific recommendations and of the comparison of different points of view, unthinkable without far-reaching publicity for the actions of the leading bodies."

He was to be denied the "far-reaching publicity" he demanded, let alone the power to initiate thoroughgoing reform, for another two years. But by hindsight it is clear that the elements of that reform were already in place in his mind.

Meanwhile, Andropov pursued reform in his own way. His

hard line began with a spectacular campaign against loaf-
ers. In broad daylight, the Militia — a branch of the police
— raided cinemas, department stores and Metro entrances,
picking up all those who had left their work without permission. The raids even netted a couple of generals who
were found in a Turkish bath during duty hours. But the
pressure was soon turned down. Punctuality at work — as
practical men like Gorbachev were quite aware — was of
little use if machines continued to run at half power, if
spares were unobtainable, and if supplies failed to arrive.

Far more successful than his theoretical and practical
attempts to spur on the labouring masses were Andropov's
moves in personnel policy. Immediately after Brezhnev's
death the November plenary meeting of the Central Committee appointed the 59-year-old Geydar Aliyev a Politburo Member and the 53-year-old Nikolai Ryzhkov a Central Committee Secretary.

Aliyev, from the Caucasus, had been for years the KGB
chief of Azerbaijan, the southern republic bordering Iran,
and subsequently First Party Secretary of the region. He
had fought the legendary corruption of Baku, the capital of
Soviet Azerbaijan and now a major port and oil centre,
with a rod of iron. In the local catch-phrase, he "restored
Soviet rule in Azerbaijan." His toughness gave rise to
countless anecdotes. It is said that even the most aggressive taxi-drivers still reduce speed when they get near his
villa, even though Aliyev now resides in Moscow. After all,
in a region historically influenced by Persian culture and
once a part of Iran, "the shah is the shah." Aliyev owed the
respect he enjoyed not only to his firmness but also to his
achievements. After he had become the Republic's Party
chief in 1969, economic growth rates in Azerbaijan, which
until then had been below the Soviet average, shot up. The
Republic's gross national product rose by 47 percent between 1975 and 1980, as against a Soviet average of only
23 percent.

To make Aliyev a Politburo Member and Deputy Premier was a shrewd move. For one thing, Aliyev, like
Andropov, had served in the KGB. For another, his promo-

tion meant that a representative of the Muslim population
moved into the centre of power (a not unimportant point in
view of developments in Iran). And finally, by bringing
Aliyev to Moscow the Party chief had gained a skilful
organizer and a man of ideas, a man to be entrusted with
one of the most urgent tasks — improvement of the dis-
astrous transport system. Since then, Aliyev has remained
one of the central figures of the new generation in the
Kremlin.

Even more important for restructuring industry was the
appointment of the new Central Committee Secretary,
Nikolai Ryzhkov. Ryzhkov had for many years been in
charge of the Soviet Union's most important industrial
complex, Uralmash, in Sverdlovsk. Now he was to set up a
new department to organize the organizers of industry —
to ensure proper liaison between the Planning Commission, the Committee for Labour and Social Affairs, and the
Committee for Price Setting. The Party was thereby hoping to go over the heads of the planning bureaucracy in the
ministries and state committees in order to achieve better
co-ordination and more effective management of industrial
activities. (Ryzhkov has remained Gorbachev's closest collaborator in his attempts to reform the Soviet economy.)

Andropov's next move — a major step in his anti-corruption campaign — came on December 17 1983, when Nikolai Shcholokov was forced out. This 72-year-old general
had once attended the Institute of Metallurgy in Dnepropetrovsk, as had Brezhnev and several other Party veterans. When Brezhnev was Party chief of Moldavia in the
early 1950's, Shcholokov had been Deputy Premier there.
Brezhnev later made his old friend his Minister of the
Interior, although Shcholokov brought neither experience
nor ability to that job. All he did was allow the Soviet
police to become a flourishing field of corruption.

That such an old friend of Brezhnev's could be overthrown so quickly was evidence of the resolution with
which Andropov's guard was moving against the Brezhnev
clan. It was also a measure of how compromising those
deals in furs, jewelery and caviar, the building of *dachas*

and the gifts to the Party must have been. Later, after Andropov's death, Shcholokov was stripped of all his military ranks, and there was nothing the new Party leader, Chernenko — as much Brezhnev's friend as Shcholokov was — could do about it. Shcholokov would have been put on trial, had he not died — by his own hand, according to the inevitable rumour.

Shcholokov's dismissal was just the beginning. Altogether nine high-ranking Brezhnev proteges lost their posts during Andropov's 13 months in office; 19 out of 84 ministers, 20 percent of all Regional Party chiefs and several Central Committee departmental heads were replaced. The purge of the Militia assumed such proportions that the new KGB chief (and present Minister of the Interior) Vitali Fedorchuk declared in *Pravda* that recruits for the police would now also have to come from the Army because the Militia had been so badly depleted by disciplinary measures. Half a dozen deputies of Shcholokov went, including Brezhnev's son-in-law Yuri Churbanov, and a host of Brezhnev's friends and supporters, including Deputy Premier Ignati Novikov, the Agit-Prop chief Tyazhelnikov, the (since deceased) Party theoretician Sergei Trapeznikov, the Minister of Railways Ivan Pavlovsky and his Deputy Nikolai Konarev. The Chairman of the State Committee for Foreign Economic Relations, Smelyakov, and one of his staff, Pavlov, were sentenced to death.

This wave of purges raises a question: What was the part played by the most important of Andropov's three pillars which supported his rise to power — the KGB? Obviously, the Security Service could not conduct the anti-corruption campaign alone. Control commissions, investigating authorities and law courts had to be involved. But it was the KGB that was the driving force behind the campaign. This role, as well as Andropov's support, made it increasingly a state within the state, giving its new leaders vastly greater influence. By fully utilizing the KGB in his drives for discipline, Andropov brought the security organization firmly in line with his goal and in the process helped to forge a de facto alliance between the KGB and

Gorbachev, Andropov's favourite candidate for the succession. Two of the top KGB men were Vitali Fedorchuk (who initially succeeded Andropov as KGB chief but shortly afterwards became Minister of the Interior) and Georgi Tsinev (who became First Deputy Chairman of the KGB in 1982). These two have always been connected with the Armed Forces in supervisory roles. For several decades they were specialists in the Chief Directorate for Counter-Espionage (GUKR) and for a long time commanded the KGB's Third Department which deals with surveillance of the Army.

Fedorchuk, who between 1944 and 1947 fought against Ukrainian nationalists, later became Head of Counter-Espionage. In 1970 he went back to the Ukraine for Brezhnev in order to suppress the renewed spirit of nationalism there and to dismiss the Ukrainian Party chief, Pyotr Shelest, who had become too much of a nationalist for Brezhnev's taste. An uncompromising persecutor of Ukrainian dissidents, Fedorchuk was brought back to Moscow by Andropov, but was switched with surprising speed from the KGB Chairmanship to the post of Minister of the Interior.

He was replaced by Viktor Chebrikov, who though an old fellow-fighter of Brezhnev from Dnepropetrovsk, had gained Andropov's confidence.

As the KGB rose in influence, the Military — the second of Brezhnev's pillars — declined. After the summer of 1983, when Andropov's physical strength was waning and military spokesmen increasingly took on the business of issuing statements and holding press conferences, there was speculation that the Military were gaining in political influence. But this was not so. Not a single general had risen in the political hierarchy, except for the special case of the then First Deputy Chief of the General Staff, Sergei Akhromeyev. At the Central Committee meetings in November 1982, in June 1983 and finally in December 1983, only one contribution came from the ranks of the Army.

Moreover, the Military had to shoulder a fearful disaster: the shooting down of the Korean KAL 007 airliner. When the Chief of the General Staff Nikolai Ogarkov was forced to appear before foreign journalists on September 9 1983 following the incident, this was the first press conference given by a Chief of the Soviet General Staff since Marshal Tukhachevsky's day. The tragedy had been the result of a terrible chain of miscalculations and mistrust by all involved, including the US and South Korea. Nevertheless the incident reflected badly on the Soviet Union, militarily, morally and in propaganda terms. It revealed grave weaknesses in the air defence system and in the command structure. It produced conflicts within the different services and resulted in disciplinary measures in the Far Eastern Command. Although the political leadership covered for the Armed Forces, its support seemed half-hearted. A gloomy "Statement by the General Secretary" of September 28 1983 repeatedly contained the formula "The Soviet leadership considers it necessary ...," emphasising the word "leadership" and avoiding mention of the Politburo, which had not been unanimous when it voted for the cover-up. In the end, the air disaster meant a reverse for those in the Military who nurtured political ambitions, allowing Andropov to keep them under his control. The brilliant but independent Ogarkov was to be dismissed a year later specifically so that he should *not* remain as a possible successor to the ailing Defence Minister Dmitri Ustinov, a Party man to the core.

Andropov fared less successfully with the third of Brezhnev's pillars, the diplomatic service, his own erstwhile domain. At the beginning of his rule, he seemed to be preparing the scenario for a new *modus vivendi* with America. Yet his disarmament proposals, though initially presented with some skill, were limited and confusing. For instance Hans-Jochen Vogel, then the German Social Democrats' leader, was told by Andropov on his visit to Moscow in January 1983 that, if the Geneva talks were successful, some of the SS-20 missiles (whose numbers were to be reduced) would be "liquidated." On April 2 Gromyko, talking to the press, insisted that the American demand for a "liquidation" of missiles "of itself rules out the possibility of agreement." The Soviet Union would instead pull the missiles under discussion back to Asia. The Army daily *Krasnaya Zvezda* (*Red Star*) thereupon paid an unusual tribute to Gromyko by carrying his press conference on its front page. But a few months later Andropov, in answer to a question on whether missiles cut back in Europe would be transferred to the east of the country, told *Pravda*: "Any such statements are notorious lies.... The principal procedure in the reduction... is to be their dismantling and annihilation."

We shall look more closely at Gromyko's role in Chapter 6, but there is no doubt that relations between Moscow and Washington were exacerbated to an exceptional degree during Andropov's final months. Strictly speaking, there was no longer an East–West conflict — only confrontation between the two superpowers. In Europe, nations on both sides of the Iron Curtain were individually moving towards each other. The Eastern campaign for rearmament crumbled. Erich Honecker, the East German Party chief, began to ease himself out of Moscow's control (a move described in detail in Chapter 8. It was to be halted only in September 1984, when the Kremlin — largely under Gorbachev's influence — resumed its dialogue with the White House).

Andropov's rule paralysed foreign policy. There was little Gorbachev could do about that yet. But at home, Andropov's withdrawal gave Gorbachev his chance. Almost independently, he took over Andropov's business. Since the first day of Andropov's rule, Gorbachev had tried to implement his patron's intentions the length and breadth of the country. Whatever cautious structural changes or harsh disciplinary measures Andropov announced, Gorbachev would put his head on the block for them. From being an agricultural expert, he became the supreme controller of the economy — and the economic balance sheet of Andropov's year in office was certainly respectable. Gorbachev championed Andropov's policy to such a degree that, in the spring of 1983, he encountered open opposition at a meeting in Belgorod.

Towards the end of September 1983, Andropov's ill-health kept him permanently in hospital. In October he had one kidney removed. From then on he was confined to a few specially equipped rooms at the Kuntsevo government hospital, almost continuously on life-support machines. In a room set up as both living and working quarters, linked to the outside world by its own telephone exchange, Andropov received only members of his family and his closest collaborators. Gorbachev acted as liaison officer between hospital and Kremlin.

His position was further strengthened by Andropov. The new Party chief had consolidated his position with the help of the proteges of the former "crown prince" Andrei Kirilenko. These men had come from heavy industry, from the State Planning Commission and from the governmental apparatus of the Russian Republic. They were therefore men of the old school and not reformers, but as opponents of Chernenko and former supporters of Kirilenko, they now transferred their loyalties to Andropov. They were the watchdogs in the anti-corruption campaign, more interested in imposing discipline than in inspiring initiative from below, but it was their commitment that enabled Gorbachev to become the General Secretary's indispensable Chief of Staff.

The close of 1983 was like no other time in Soviet history. The plenary meeting of the Central Committee, due under the statutes, was postponed to the last week of December. There were two reasons for this: the tug-of-war over personnel and Andropov's continuing hope that he might yet appear before the Party for a last time. In the end he had to inform the Central Committee that he was "for the moment not in a position" to attend in person.

Nevertheless the plenary meeting was a victory for the sick man. His supporters recorded their greatest triumph since Andropov had come to power. No such constellation or coalition had ever been seen before. With the installation of Vitali Vorotnikov and Mikhail Solomentsev as new Politburo Members and of Yegor Ligachev as Central Committee Secretary, Andropov's guard triumphed not only

over Chernenko's old power-base, but also over the Armed
Forces. Speculations about Chief of General Staff Ogarkov's irresistible rise to the Politburo turned out to have
been premature. True, an Army General, Viktor Chebrikov, did move up to be a Candidate Member of the Politburo — but as KGB chief, not as a military man.

Where did those men come from who moved into the
centre of power, and who today flank Gorbachev at the top
of the hierarchy?

The new Politburo Member Vitali Vorotnikov, 57 at the
time, had been one of Kirilenko's followers. When
Kirilenko's star sank, Vorotnikov — until then Deputy
Premier of the Russian Republic — was shunted off to
Cuba as ambassador in 1979. A graduate aircraft construc-
tion engineer, he was able to return to Moscow again only
when Andropov seized power, taking part in the assault on
Brezhnev and Chernenko. He cleaned up the southern
Russian province of Krasnodar after its Party chief Sergei
Medunov, a friend of Brezhnev's, had been overthrown by
Andropov. By June 1983 Vorotnikov had taken over the
important post of Premier of the Russian Republic, exercis-
ing vital influence over industry and agriculture.

The other addition to the Politburo, Mikhail
Solomentsev, already 70 in 1983, was respected for his
political skills. Belonging to the Russian national wing of
the Party, he had for years remained a Politburo Candidate Member having always been an opponent of Brezhnev. The son of peasants, he had been sent to Kazakhstan
as Second Party Secretary by Brezhnev's rival Frol Kozlov,
who had temporarily succeeded in dislodging Brezhnev's
friend, Kazakh Party chief Dinmukhamed Kunayev. When
Brezhnev came to power in 1964 he immediately went to
Kazakhstan to reappoint Kunayev and dispatch
Solomentsev and others into the wilderness. Solomentsev
became Party Secretary in Rostov, and by 1971 — assisted
by the Russites around Mikhail Suslov — worked his way
up to become Premier of the Russian Republic. But in
contrast to all his predecessors in this post, he never became a full Member of the Politburo — Brezhnev, Kunayev

and their allies blocked this step up. In June 1983 Solomentsev handed over the chairmanship of the Russian Republic's government to Vorotnikov and himself took on the Party Central Committee.

The new Central Committee Secretary, Yegor Ligachev (see also Appendix 2), 63 when he assumed this post, had taken over the chairmanship of the important Central Committee Department for Party Organization Work (the Party's personnel office, as it were) in April 1983, replacing the old Brezhnev supporter Ivan Kapitonov. Until Ligachev suddenly appeared in this post in the spring of 1983, coming in from the cold — actually from Tomsk in Siberia, where he had spent the previous 18 years — this energetic man had been virtually unknown to Kremlin watchers. But not to Andropov, who had clearly had his eye on Ligachev for some time. He had run the West Siberian oil and gas region well, had good ideas on how to improve regional structures, and had good contacts with the Siberian branch of the Academy of Sciences.

These changes in personnel were Andropov's most important legacy to Gorbachev. They opened the Kremlin gate to the younger guard. Brezhnev's proteges now found themselves confronted by disciplinarians and specialists. It was with these men that Gorbachev finally came to power.

While the world continued its guessing game as to whether Andropov — officially suffering no more than a cold — would ever return to his post, there appeared another of those oracular statements buried in a press article that hinted at what was really happening at the centre of power. On January 20–23, *Izvestiya* published a three-part series on the 60th anniversary of Lenin's death. The article on January 21 had the significant headline "Parting" and contained these highly suggestive sentences: "Even after December 12, when his illness had established its inescapable hold on him and finally tied him to his bed, Vladimir Ilyich continued to reflect on business. He was still hoping to appear before the All-Russian Congress of Soviets, he was courageously thinking a few months ahead and considering what he should say to the delegates of the 12th Party Congress. But he was not destined to accomplish this."

The parallel was clear. The semi-paralysed Lenin in Gorki was the sick Andropov in Kuntsevo hospital. And the message was equally clear. Andropov was still following events, undismayed, looking to the future — after all, he had written his report for the postponed Central Committee plenary meeting — but he would not be returning.

Andropov died on February 9 1984. He was a man of transition, but he himself shaped and promoted that transition. He built the bridge by which a new generation might come to power over the swamp of corruption. That was his achievement, one that was much underrated in the West merely because he did not live up to Western preconceptions of him as a liberal reformer. But then to measure Soviet attempts at reform solely by the yardstick of Western democratic ideas is a barren exercise — a point worth remembering in any assessment of Soviet leaders, including Gorbachev.

6

A "Second General Secretary"

After Andropov's death, there were two candidates for the office of General Secretary, candidates who could not be more different. The young, self-assured, competent Gorbachev, standing for a radical overhaul of the Soviet system, for efficiency, for incentives, for agricultural reforms, and for a new guiding mechanism for the economy; and the aging, uncertain Chernenko, offering a return to tranquillity and conservatism.

The correct choice seemed obvious. Yet the majority of the Party leadership decided in Chernenko's favour. Why?

The answer provides a curious insight both into the workings of the Politburo and into Gorbachev's own character.

The decision was controversial. Although Andropov had long been terminally ill and although there were indications in Moscow that the Politburo had designated Chernenko as the future General Secretary some time before, the nomination of Brezhnev's old friend as Chairman of the Funeral Commission — a first step to his formal appointment as General Secretary — was not announced until two days after Andropov's death on February 9. Four days later, on February 13, the plenary meeting of the Central Committee approved Premier Tikhonov's proposal that

Chernenko be elected the new General Secretary.

At the time, reports in the Soviet press suggested this was routine. Yet 48 hours later it became obvious that the press had withheld a significant piece of information. On February 15, a special release about the plenary meeting revealed that there had been a very unusual closing speech. The meeting was wound up not, as would have been normal, by the new General Secretary, but by Mikhail Gorbachev.

Gorbachev's speech and the fact that it was concealed by the press revealed three things. Firstly, there was clearly a strong feeling in favour of leadership passing to the younger generation, as represented by Gorbachev. Secondly, Chernenko and his followers tried to avoid humiliation by keeping this lack of unanimity from the public. Thirdly, Gorbachev went along with them. In other words, there was a deal between the generations. Gorbachev was consecrated as the "crown prince," and in return the Old Guard was allowed to bow out gracefully. Although Gorbachev avoided any kind of praise for the new General Secretary in his final address, he did appeal to that "spirit of unity and solidarity which has characterized this Central Committee plenary meeting." And the arrangement did indeed hold throughout the year of Chernenko's weak reign. That it did so was to the credit of the collective leadership in the Kremlin, and evidence of a greater readiness to compromise.

But why was such a deal necessary? Why should the Party summit decide once again to put the clock back, to choose aged infirmity over youthful good health, to replace Andropov — who had been so chronically ill that he could not even take the October Revolution Parade in 1983 — with a man who was three years older and suffering from the lung complaint emphysema so badly that it had already compelled his absence from the 1983 observance of Lenin's birthday and the May Day procession?

Several reasons clearly emerged:

Firstly, confronted by Andropov's reformist zeal, the veterans were anxious about their privileges and benefits, and their proteges were anxious about their positions. Chernenko would reduce the pace;

Secondly, many top officials of the older generation, still terrified by the lesson of the Khrushchev era, feared that sudden change might lead to a loss of control, to a weakening of planning, to a thaw, to a host of unpredictable consequences. Chernenko would provide stability;

Thirdly, the provincial barons in the Politburo regarded Moscow's orders to mend their ways as interference in their regional sovereignty. The Kazakh Party chief Din-mukhamed Kunayev, for instance, an old friend of Brezhnev and Chernenko, had been forced to dismiss one-third of his Party Secretaries. The First Party Secretary of the Ukraine, Politburo Member Vladimir Shcherbitsky, had lost nine of his 25 regional Party chiefs as a result of Andropov's corruption campaign. The Moscow City Party chief, Viktor Grishin, had been particularly badly hit by Andropov's purge. The huge scandal about Gastronom No. 1, the economic offences among the friends of Brezhnev's daughter Galina, and the unseating of one in three top officials in the capital — all this had gravely damaged Grishin's standing. Chernenko would not undermine the power of the provincial chiefs;

And finally, there was a certain sense of solidarity with the old, grey servant of the Party. For 30 years, Chernenko had clung to Brezhnev's coat-tails, only to be embarrassed by the revelations about Brezhnev's corrupt clique. Chernenko deserved better.

But how could Chernenko, Brezhnev's loyal squire, a man whose concept of the world was based on provincial agit-prop, be expected to guide the destinies of a world power? Chernenko had been taken along by Brezhnev on a few visits abroad, to socialist countries and Third World states. (What a contrast to Gorbachev's performances in Canada, Britain and Italy!) But he had never taken much notice of the rest of the world. Chernenko's professional experience was confined to supervising the mills of bureaucracy. As Brezhnev's political valet, he had learned how to manipulate the system unnoticed by the decision-makers within the Party. He was the champion of all those who feared Andropov's and Gorbachev's reforms.

Although Chernenko stood for more consumer goods and greater prosperity — in this, at any rate, he was united with Gorbachev against the rearmament lobby — he stuck to the old ideas of appealing directly to the masses. The promotion of group interests and wage differentials as incentives to improve efficiency seemed to him economically risky and politically suspect. He stood for the preservation of the unspoken agreement between the two sides of industry, an agreement once explained to me in these words: "Why should our workers rise up against the system so long as, day after day, they can make something from their work-place walk home with them?"

In his 35-minute inaugural address to the Central Committee plenary meeting on February 13 1984, the new General Secretary obliquely warned against pressures for reform, efficiency or discipline. Creation of new economic structures demanded a great deal of responsibility. In that connection one was well advised to remember the old Russian proverb: "Measure seven times, cut once." Besides, in making any essential decisions one should "listen to the words that come from the workers."

To speak for these workers, to be listened to by them — that had always been Chernenko's wish. Now he was practising just that, from the top level, heavy-handedly, never able to escape the legacy of his peasant background. He was born under the Tsar, in 1911, in the central Siberian village of Bolshaya Tes. At 18, he embarked on his Party career as leader of the local Komsomol. In 1931, the year Gorbachev was born, the year Stalin's campaign for the "liquidation of the kulaks as a class" reached its climax, Chernenko joined the Party. The 1930's, the years in which Stalin staged his show trials, are missing from Chernenko's biography. Grim but unconfirmed reports claim that, as an NKVD (Secret Police) officer in Brezhnev's home town of Dnepropetrovsk, Chernenko took an active part in Stalin's bloody purges. Chernenko was one of the few top-level officials of his generation not to see frontline service during the Great Patriotic War. The only explanation for this appears in a brief, embarrassed note in the preface to the English edition of his speeches: "Nazi Germany's attack on my country found me in the post of Secretary of the Krasnoyarsk Territorial Party Committee. I immediately volunteered for frontline duty but my requests were turned down."

After the war Brezhnev made Chernenko his ADC. Chernenko was his agit-prop chief when, in the early 1950's, Brezhnev was the Party chief in Moldavia, formerly part of Romania. Closely linked to the Brezhnev clique, Chernenko was politically compromised before he was elected leader. It had been the same in the ailing tsarist empire. "Fear and loathing of liberal ideas," Alexander Herzen wrote in the middle of the last century, "were so great that the government could no longer reconcile itself to civilization.... Gigantic efforts were made to preserve an artificial state of tranquillity. Yet absolutism for the sake of absolutism is impossible in the long run: it is too nonsensical and too barren."

"Absolutism for the sake of absolutism is nonsensical" — this was what Gorbachev had believed ever since his student days and what had led him to collaborate with Andropov. The end only occasionally justified the means; to him, politics and power were not in themselves sacred. To drown socialism in a sea of tranquillity seemed to him not only nonsensical but also incompatible with the interests of his nation and the needs of its people.

As the official No. 2 in the Party, Gorbachev made it immediately and publicly clear that he intended to press on with Andropov's policy. His slogan was: "Everything that is new and progressive must be consolidated and multiplied — we have no alternative" (*Izvestiya*, March 1 1984). His "private army" was standing by, and revealed itself immediately after Chernenko's accession.

In the election speeches for the Supreme Soviet on March 4 1984, this co-ordinated group hammered home the central points: positive change had started with the first Central Committee meeting under Andropov in November 1982; 1983 had been the turning-point; the task now was to improve labour discipline and management even further.

Politburo Member Vitali Vorotnikov was quoted as saying: "Important measures have recently been taken to strengthen order and discipline, to eliminate work losses, and to act more effectively against violators of labour discipline. These measures have met with truly universal approval by the people, they have not only had a positive effect on indices but also fortified the moral health of society. It is important that concern for these issues does not diminish." On the same occasion, Central Committee Secretary Yegor Ligachev, who in his role as Andropov's new personnel chief had pensioned off so many of Brezhnev's favourites that he could not expect any favours from Chernenko anyway, phrased his attack on the Old Guard obliquely but unambiguously: "Young people, of course, are our future — but they are also our present," and then asserted that there was still much to be done: "It would be a mistake to overestimate what we have achieved so far." But it was Central Committee Secretary Nikolai Ryzhkov who showed his antagonism towards Chernenko more clearly than anyone else. He disregarded Kremlin ritual by only briefly mentioning Chernenko's appointment as General Secretary, and by omitting a tribute to his leadership qualities. In the coded language of the Kremlin, this disdainful treatment of the new leader was downright offensive.

The reminders by Gorbachev's men that the economic successes of 1983 should be underpinned by even more discipline and efficiency were not of course echoed by the Old Guard members around the new General Secretary. Instead, over the next few months, Chernenko's followers pleaded, indirectly, for moderation in the speed of change. Brezhnev's daughter Galina suddenly reappeared. On March 8 she was invited to the Kremlin in connection with Women's Day. Yuri Churbanov was allowed to return from his exile in Murmansk. The economic situation was described in mild and smug terms. Under Andropov, the word "discipline" had had overtones of a threat of disciplinary measures. Chernenko's propagandists spoke reassuringly of "conscious discipline," implying that nothing harsh would be imposed from above. Threats invoking the "organs" of security became calls for more "organization."

As for foreign policy, the new General Secretary seemed to take part in this only for the sake of form. At his first major international meeting, with the Ethiopian head of state Mengistu Haile Mariam, Chernenko was flanked by other Politburo Members — Ustinov, Gromyko and Aliyev. On a visit to India, Defence Minister Ustinov publicly conveyed not only the greetings of the General Secretary (as protocol demanded) but also those of the Premier and Foreign Minister. Aliyev did the same in Syria.

In the early summer Chernenko disappeared from the political stage. For some time, he had been seen publicly moving laboriously and with breathing difficulties along the rows of the Supreme Soviet. He remained absent for many weeks, staying at the north Caucasian spa of Mineralnye Vody, in Gorbachev's native region, to ease his breathing and circulation.

When Chernenko left Moscow that summer, the Soviet Union's diplomatic isolation, intensified by Foreign Minister Gromyko, reached its peak. Relations with the United States were frozen as a result of the Soviet boycott of the Los Angeles Olympics. A long-planned visit to China by Vice-Premier Arkhipov was high-handedly cancelled, placing a heavy strain on already difficult relations with Peking. The Warsaw Pact countries all showed unprecedented independence. Anxious about the threat to the policy of detente and the economic effects of this threat, East Germany, Hungary, Bulgaria and Romania all openly opposed the Soviet armament programme, and the arms race in general. A vague vision of a "European community of responsibility" emerged. The East German and Bulgarian leaders, Erich Honecker and Todor Zhivkov, insisted on making planned visits to Bonn against Moscow's objection.

Not only was Chernenko missing from Moscow at this time but Foreign Minister Gromyko was also absent, on his holidays. The Kremlin's business was shared by Gorbachev and the 75-year-old Defence Minister, Dmitri Ustinov. When Ustinov paid a visit to Czechoslovakia that summer, it was Gorbachev who saw him off and welcomed him back. On previous occasions, this seemingly trivial chore had been undertaken by Politburo Member Grigori Romanov who, as Central Committee Secretary, was closely concerned with military—industrial interests. In the context of Soviet politics, these subtle shifts often carry major significance.

In September there appeared in the Soviet press hints of things to come. On September 2, the daily *Sovetskaya Rossiya* published a front-page article about the death at the age of 73 of Lenin's mother. "At that age any sickness might strike a person," the paper observed. Chernenko's 73rd birthday was due to fall that month. On September 4, *Pravda* carried an editorial on the preparations for the 27th Party Congress, to be held in February 1986. No mention was made of Chernenko, although in theory he would be working on the new Party programme to be adopted by that Congress. This was a deliberate (and, as it turned out, correct) hint that Chernenko would not be working on preparations for the Congress and that they were already being handled by someone else — Gorbachev.

These hints were all the more pointed since it was on September 5 that Chernenko was due to make his first public appearance, after an absence of 53 days. The occasion was specially arranged and then rearranged to suit him. He hobbled into the Kremlin's ceremonial hall to present medals to three cosmonauts, who had actually completed their mission on July 29, five weeks previously. Standing utterly rigid, the Party chief managed to endure the 20-minute ceremony. At the end, in an expressionless voice and breathing with just as much difficulty as before his spa treatment, he staggered through his five-minute address.

Everything seemed to be back to where it was before.

The General Secretary and his policies seemed destined to drag on into the autumn unchanged. However, on the following day, September 6, a bald sentence came ticking over the Tass teleprinter, causing perplexity, confusion and wild speculation in the West. The sentence ran: "Marshal of the Soviet Union N.V. Ogarkov has been relieved of his post of Chief of the General Staff of the Soviet Armed Forces and of First Deputy Minister of Defence in connection with his assumption of another task."

The dismissal of the 66-year-old Ogarkov, a highly gifted but independent-minded man, who was viewed as a possible future Defence Minister, was the most serious assault on the military hierarchy by the political leadership since Khrushchev sacked his Defence Minister, Marshal Zhukov, in 1957. Among all the speculation about the meaning of this move, two factors stood out. Firstly, Gorbachev and Ustinov had, during the preceding weeks been in close political collaboration; and secondly, at the time Ogarkov was relieved of his office Gorbachev's rival Grigori Romanov, the man responsible in the Party leadership for military and industrial matters, was on a prolonged tour of Ethiopia. Clearly, the Ogarkov affair related to the appointment of a successor to Defence Minister Ustinov who had been ailing for some time. The obvious candidate, Ogarkov, whose alliegance was never clear, had now been jettisoned.

One surprise was followed by another. Simultaneously with Ogarkov's dismissal, there was an equally startling U-turn in foreign policy. Andrei Gromyko suddenly announced that he would be visiting President Reagan at the White House on September 28. Until then, Gromyko's policy had been consistently negative on contacts with the US — a total refusal of any dialogue with Washington, as a reprisal for Reagan's crusading anti-Soviet militancy. Certainly, no one would have thought a visit possible before the American elections in November.

Why the about-turn? To persuade the West Europeans to oppose Reagan's Star Wars programme and to placate the

East Europeans — a matter of considerable urgency, for it was in large measure Gromyko's intransigence that caused the Eastern Bloc countries to talk of a "European community of responsibility." The Soviet Union wanted a new start, to lead its own camp again, and to court Western Europe with diplomatic efforts for a reduction in the arms race. There was to be a show of readiness for dialogue, without any substantial change of line — just what the Americans had long been doing in their dealings with their Western allies.

But how had this sudden change of direction in the Kremlin come about? Had the collective leadership performed this manoeuvre overnight in perfect concord? Or had there been differences and compromises? Was Ogarkov's sacking somehow connected with the about-turn in foreign policy?

While the process by which the policy change occurred is unclear, it seems certain that Gorbachev played a decisive part in effecting the change. He had repeatedly spoken of the international situation with more confidence and in a more conciliatory spirit than other Politburo Members. In June 1984, while he was investing the city of Smolensk with the Order of Lenin, he became the first Politburo Member to hint at a new readiness to talk. "The Soviet Union is committed to an honest dialogue with genuine content," he said, "to serious negotiations on the basis of equality and equal security."

In September 1984 in Sofia, Bulgaria, he clearly enunciated the outlines of a new policy that affected both East–West relations and relations with other Warsaw Pact countries. Speaking from the platform of the Dimitrov Mausoleum near the Russian Boulevard, on the 40th anniversary of the communist seizure of power, he did not indulge in the usual references to the war. Instead, he expressed a touch of regret about the deterioration of East–West relations, studiously avoiding the familiar litany of Cold War platitudes. He promised the Bulgarians, who had long feared Soviet rearmament on their own territory, a nuclear-free zone in the Balkans. He then persuaded the

Bulgarian Party chief Zhivkov, who had just succeeded in gaining an invitation to West Germany, to cancel his visit. Zhivkov, he promised, had no need to go, for the Soviet Union would smooth the way for a new East–West relationship.

There is no doubt that Chernenko also supported the decision to resume negotiations to slow down the arms race. But where did Foreign Minister Gromyko stand?

Gromyko's position was extraordinary. Never before had any Russian foreign minister had such authority. After Andropov's death, for the first time in history, a foreign minister, virtually unchecked, controlled Russia's global destiny. And while he held the reins in his hands, he seemed to have but one objective: to bury detente as speedily as possible, to bury it just as eagerly as President Reagan. Gromyko — "grim Grom," the man with the hangdog look — became Reagan's antagonist.

Rigid to the point of obduracy, flexible only when forced to be, Gromyko was a past-master of Soviet foreign policy. His career began in the war when Stalin, realizing the Soviet Union had an opportunity to become a world power, determined to secure for his country an extensive buffer zone in Central Europe. In 1943 Gromyko became ambassador in Washington. Then in Teheran, Yalta and Potsdam, Gromyko helped to secure the Soviet Union's territorial gains with international treaties. Those accretions he subsequently protected against collapse as the post-war empire's roving trouble-shooter.

To the West, he seemed much more a man of the world than most other top officials — quiet, reserved, but never servile. Even Khrushchev at his most offensive could not dispel his long-suffering Buster Keaton expression. Once Gromyko listened to Khrushchev boasting of his authority. "If I invited Gromyko to take off his trousers", Khrushchev said, "and sit down on a block of ice, then he would do so." Gromyko remained impassive, his eyes, in Henry Kissinger's words, "slightly wistful like those of a dog that has to endure some intolerable affront from his master."

Gromyko rose from being Stalin's "Mr. Nyet," the man who said nothing but "No" in the Security Council, to become the principal Soviet architect of the treaty with West Germany by which both countries renounced the use of force. But in the late 1970's, Gromyko reverted increasingly to his role as "Mr. Nyet."

His rigidity was missed at first by many observers, simply because Gromyko was so familiar as the Kremlin's only regular "Western salesman." His experience was awe-inspiring, his memory phenomenal. "Any idea what's become of poor Thomsen?" Gromyko once asked a Bonn diplomat who prided himself on his knowledge of history. The diplomat shook his head. Who was Thomsen? He was a German secretary in Washington in 1940, whom Gromyko had met as a young counsellor. That was the world in which Gromyko was at home. The truth was though that he was out of touch. His daughter Emilia, according to Shevchenko, once remarked: "My father is living up in the clouds. For the past 26 years he has not set foot in a Moscow street. All he sees is the view from his car window."

At the peak of his personal influence, Gromyko's policy seemed to founder on the very qualities that had underpinned his career for decades. His phenomenal memory and his presence of mind could no longer offset his lack of flexibility, imagination and vision. Diplomacy was all he knew. But Soviet foreign policy was now governed by domestic needs, and diplomatic sleight of hand was of secondary value. Gromyko had never learned to develop his own thinking. The sum total of his experience led him to rely not on innovation but only on the passage of time. But time was now running out for the declining Soviet empire, and for Gromyko.

During Andropov's and Chernenko's time in office, Gromyko had on several occasions adopted a harder line than his bosses. In the summer of 1984, during Chernenko's absence, Gromyko once more appeared to be at odds with his own government. On June 29, Tass released a government statement asserting "the need for immediate measures to prevent the militarization of space," and proposing Soviet–American negotiations in Vienna in September. A few days later, on July 2, at a dinner for the British Foreign Secretary, Sir Geoffrey Howe, Gromyko said that the Americans had rejected the suggestion with a counter-proposal that "negotiations about space should be combined with those on nuclear medium-range weapons in Europe and with those on strategic armaments." This was eventually accepted, but at the time Gromyko declared the American suggestion to be a "negative answer," and rejected it in his turn, apparently ending the dialogue between the superpowers. Yet on July 6, Tass issued a statement reversing Gromyko's stand, keeping the lines of communication open.

Quite evidently, this was the opening skirmish in a struggle that ended the following month with Gromyko going to Washington and finally making him accept the Geneva negotiations on all three types of weapons.

For Gromyko, this was the beginning of the end.

In expressing his unexpected readiness to talk to the United States, Chernenko seemed fortified. He grandly outlined to American journalists and Western politicians the unlimited possibilities of armament controls of all kinds. Gorbachev vanished from the public eye for a surprisingly long time, cancelling some meetings (including one with Labour leader Neil Kinnock on November 26) and staying away from others.

On October 23 at a Central Committee plenary meeting to discuss agriculture, Chernenko made another efforts to save Brezhnev's legacy by announcing a "Long-Term Programme for Land Improvement and for Increased Efficiency in the Utilization of Improved Land with a View to a Steady Increase in the Country's Food Supplies." In this he pleaded for an increase in production based on all the old recipes — cost-intensive land reclamation, gigantic irrigation schemes, spectacular stock-breeding projects.

As it happened, Gorbachev had already scotched any chance of this unrealistic programme being put into effect by holding his own agricultural conference seven months before, at which he proclaimed that what was lacking was not new land but new management.He said quite simply that more had to be produced "from available land and with available equipment." Nevertheless, although Gorbachev had in effect criticized everything Chernenko was saying, he kept silent.

Three weeks after the plenary meeting on agriculture, the Old Guard tried to demonstrate once more that Chernenko and his allies continued to lay down political guidelines. On November 15, there was a highly unusual meeting of the Politburo. Chernenko summoned all the provincial barons among the Politburo Members, let every participant have his say, and himself gave a report entitled "Accelerate the Intensification of the Economy," a report unambiguously following Brezhnev's and not Andropov's line. The list of speakers and Chernenko's report immediately appeared in the press, although it was then the practice that nothing was ever published about Politburo meetings other than empty communiques. The purpose of this publicity was to make clear that a small economic summit had been held — in the absence of the Central Committee Secretary responsible for the supervision of the economy, Gorbachev, and in the absence of his ally, Vitali Vorotnikov. Accordingly, these two should no longer be regarded as indispensable. Whether the men were on leave or otherwise prevented from attending, the point of the message could only be this: Chernenko was the one who made the decisions.

On December 10 1984 in the "House of Political Education" of the Moscow City Soviet, Gorbachev made a statement full of significant demands — a modification of centralism, a stronger emphasis on group interests, a change in the Party's propaganda methods — but *Pravda* did not publicize half of what Gorbachev said.

Some Western commentators assumed his star was suddenly on the wane. They overlooked the fact that Gorbachev could by now well afford that kind of modesty. He had accumulated more power and posts than any other No. 2 in the Party ever had — including Suslov. On paper, of

course, the sick General Secretary was still his superior.
But in his role of Central Committee Secretary Gorbachev
now controlled ideology, the Party machine, the economy
and agriculture. This gave him supreme supervision over
six of the nine Central Committee Secretaries. Two of them
were old allies: Ryzhkov (Economic Department) and
Ligachev (Cadre Department). The Central Committee
Secretaries Rusakov (Department for Socialist Countries),
Kapitonov (Light Industry) and Zimyanin (Propaganda
and Culture), while not siding with Gorbachev, had only
slight influence. The same was true of Boris Ponomarev
(Department for International Relations, likewise part of
the ideological sphere), who years after Khrushchev's revelations about Stalin still had the dictator's portrait
hanging in his office. Gorbachev's closest allies also included Nikolai Kruchina (Head of the Central Committee
Department for the Organization of Party Work), Vladimir
Karlov (Agricultural and Foodstuffs Industry), Venyamin
Afonin (Chemical Industry) and Vadim Medvedev (Educational and Scientific Institutions).

Gorbachev's rival, Grigori Romanov, the Central Com-
mittee Secretary responsible for the defence industry and
administration, controlled only the Central Committee
Secretary for Heavy Industry (then Vladimir Dolgikh).
And he shared with Gorbachev top-level responsibility for
Nikolai Ryzhkov's Secretariat (Economic Department).

Viktor Afanasyev, the editor-in-chief of *Pravda*, gave an
accurate description of the actual state of affairs to the
Japanese newspaper *Asahi Shimbun* on October 9 1984.
Gorbachev, he said, was practically the "second General
Secretary" of the Party.

The remark caused astonishment in the West for there
was no such post. But Gorbachev was the man for it,
nevertheless. The year under Chernenko was lost time for
the economy (as the statistics published in early 1985
showed) but not for the "second General Secretary." Gorbachev was able to develop his qualities of leadership without having to assume full responsibility. When he kept
silent at Chernenko's agricultural conference, he was not

in retreat; he was biding his time. Soon, Chernenko's bombastic and extravagant programme disappeared from the headlines. Top-level officials in their election speeches for the Soviet parliaments in February 1985 disregarded it altogether. It was not even mentioned in *Pravda's* retrospective article on Chernenko's first year in office.

For a year, Gorbachev harboured his talents for resolute action, for tactical manoeuvring, for waiting. He would need them all soon enough.

7

Gorbachev in Power

Gorbachev's aims before his accession were of course well known to those who had to decide on the succession. The lines were clearly drawn: the old Brezhnev clan, supported by ministries and the planning bureaucracy on the one hand and the inheritors of Andropov supported by the KGB on the other.

But the struggle was by no means straightforward, notwithstanding the deal between the generations. The Old Guard sought to cancel the settlement of the succession made in Gorbachev's favour, the most public evidence of this being the embarrassing sight of an ailing Chernenko on television casting his vote for the parliamentary elections, supported by the Moscow Party chief, Viktor Grishin, himself a contender for the succession.

Then, on the day of Chernenko's death, Gorbachev's opponents again attempted to retain control. According to the official bulletin, the Secretary General died at 19.20 hours on March 10 1985. At around 22.30 hours the Soviet Party leadership gathered. Of the ten Politburo Members, three — Vladimir Shcherbitsky (who was in the USA), Vitali Vorotnikov (in Yugoslavia) and the Party chief of Kazakhstan, Dinmukhamed Kunayev — could not get to Moscow on time; nor could Candidate Member and Geor-

gian Party leader Eduard Shevardnadze. At this meeting,
Gorbachev's leading opponent, Grigori Romanov, proposed
the 70-year-old Viktor Grishin as the new General Secretary.

Thereupon, it was Gromyko who first pleaded for Gorbachev. The man who was now elected would have to lead
the Soviet Union into the new millennium, he said. If that
was not thought important, then, after all, why not suggest
himself as a candidate? After Gromyko, the KGB Chairman Viktor Chebrikov closed the ranks in favour of Gorbachev, pointing to Grishin's failure to tackle the corruption that was rife in Moscow among Galina's circle of
friends.

The next day, at the Plenum of the Central Committee
meeting to elect the new General Secretary, only some 200
of the 300 representatives arrived in time. Several senior
diplomats and regional Party chiefs were not able to make
the journey. Shcherbitsky was still on his way back from
the United States. Again, Gromyko proposed Gorbachev.
As neither the Party leadership nor the Central Committee Plenum were completely gathered, Gorbachev was
voted in "nem. con." (and not "unanimously").

The hurried inauguration, in effect by-passing the Central Committee (the highest body between the Party Congresses), was not only the result of the new leadership
wishing to demonstrate their dynamism. It was also designed to prevent any opposition, however limited, forming
in the Central Committee, riddled as it was with old Brezhnev supporters and the Military. Hence also the gloss of
normality — Gromyko and France's visiting Foreign
Minister Roland Dumas met as planned, and lunched
together. Shortly thereafter the Plenary Session began. A
little later that afternoon, the aged Prime Minister, Nikolai Tikhonov, received Dumas. At 18.09 hours Moscow
time the election of Gorbachev was made public.

The details of the Plenum, however, were not immediately revealed. Gromyko's speech was not reported in
the Soviet papers, though a similar speech by Chernenko
(for Andropov's election in 1982) and Tikhonov (for Cher-

nenko's election in 1984) had been published verbatim. The reason for this mystery became apparent only a week later. Gromyko had extemporized his speech. Moreover, although noted for his bone-dry style, Gromyko had to speak with unusual vehemence to persuade certain groups to agree to Gorbachev's election.

Gromyko described Gorbachev as the man who had brilliantly chaired Politburo meetings in the absence of Chernenko. Gorbachev had a keen intellect, Gromyko said, and was a man of principle and firm convictions. "Comrades, this man has a nice smile," said Gromyko, in words that were soon to become wellknown, "but he has teeth of iron." As if it were necessary to counter doubts about Gorbachev's competence and toughness in external affairs, Gromyko added, "Perhaps because of my official responsibilities, it is rather clearer to me than to other comrades that he can grasp very well and very quickly the essence of those developments that are building up outside our country in the international arena. I myself have often been surprised by his ability to distinguish quickly and exactly the heart of a matter and to draw the right conclusions in the interests of the Party." Gromyko also defended Gorbachev's directness with unusual energy. Should anyone be put in poor humour by such openness, said the veteran diplomat, then he could not be considered "a true communist."

It is ironic to recall these words today. Gromyko could hardly have guessed when he so vociferously championed Gorbachev that the new leader would make short work both of him and his policy. Four months after Gorbachev's accession, Gromyko went into semi-retirement, shunted upstairs to become Head of State.

Following Gorbachev's election, the opposition collapsed. Previously, Soviet Party chiefs had generally required years to consolidate their power. Gorbachev, however, was firmly in the saddle immediately, appointing trusted confidants to key positions. Before the end of 1985 he was to remove 16 of the Soviet Union's 64 ministers and replace about 20 percent of local Party officials.

How far do Gorbachev's opportunities really extend? To

what extent does the beginning of his rule differ from that of his predecessors? Some conclusions emerge by examining five major issues: Gorbachev's style in his dealings with the public and the Party; his campaigns against alcohol and corruption; his attitude to the recent past, in particular to Stalin, with whose autocratic ways Gorbachev's own forceful manner has been compared; his new personnel; and the consequences of the dramatic changes.

The Great Communicator

On May 17 1985, Gorbachev donned the mantle of Lenin. The place he chose was laden with significance — Leningrad's Smolny Institute, once the command post of the Military Revolutionary Committee, where in 1917 Lenin had proclaimed the victory of Bolshevism. Now Gorbachev stood on the same spot, leaning on the delicate white balustrade and gesturing lightly with his right hand. Above him loomed a massive portrait of Lenin.

Other men in that situation might have seemed overshadowed. But not Gorbachev.

Dressed in a well-cut dark blue suit, Gorbachev pressed for a new beginning: "We must all change our attitudes, from the worker to the minister, the Secretary of the Central Committee and the leaders of the government.... We must naturally give all our cadres a chance, but anyone who is not prepared to do so must simply get out of our way and must not be allowed to interfere."

The words were spoken quietly, even mildly. But the toughness of the content became clear later. By "the Secretary of the Central Committee" Gorbachev meant his rival, Politburo Member and former Leningrad Party chief Grigori Romanov. Only a few weeks later, Romanov had to "get out of the way," forced into retirement without a single word to honour his contribution.

But for the great majority in the hall of the Smolny Institute on that May afternoon, this speech — or rather the style of its delivery — proclaimed something of far greater importance. It contained none of the usual pseudo-revolutionary bombast, no melodramatic paeans to a glorious future, no promises of new wealth, no dry statistics. This was no grey bureaucrat clinging rigidly to the lectern, reciting the empty rhetoric of his speechwriters. Here was a spellbinding orator, varying pace and tone like an actor. At one moment he played the executive, counting off on his fingers how much more a rouble was worth if instead of being invested in energy production it went into conservation; then he used charm, chatting informally with his hand in his pocket; then once again he became the stern, lecturing expert, stabbing a finger at the auditorium. One moment he rolled his fists, arms bent, to describe the better work rhythms that he desired, and the next, in muted and intimate tones, his words punctuated with pauses and smiles, he wooed his listeners until they were no longer aware of his southern accent and the occasional lapse into rural syntax.

This performance, and the selection of Leningrad as the venue, contained all the elements of his "new style" — the dramatic delivery, the subtle questioning of old ideas with carefully modified emphases, and the symbolic use of setting, stance and style of speech.

For many who were there, it was as though the old Smolny Institute was experiencing its second historic performance in this century — first Lenin, then Gorbachev. Never before had a leader spoken to them in this manner. Three days later, TV viewers were equally spellbound. For Gorbachev's Leningrad performance was broadcast with only minor editing at prime time. Although he did not have much of substance to say about concrete changes (he spoke of "economic reform," a phrase usually avoided, but he did so only in connection with East Germany), the country was fascinated.

What lay behind this dramatic speech? Because of its significance, Gorbachev's journey to Leningrad bears closer examination. He had two motives, one symbolic, the other practical.

The old St. Petersburg was the window to the West that

Peter the Great had pushed open. Lenin moved the seat of the new rulers back to Moscow again, into the old centre that had for centuries gathered around itself an enormous bulwark of imperial lands protecting Russia's leaders from the West. But Leningrad still retained its European flavour. The St. Petersburg/Leningrad tradition was only ended when Stalin turned Russia's back on the world to achieve "socialism in one country." Gorbachev's trip recalled the European tradition, evoking those more open-minded rulers who sought renewal with the help of Western ideas.

Moreover, the trip also served to emphasise the type of changes Gorbachev wished to initiate. He and Raisa, besides making a point of visiting monuments of the old St. Petersburg, paid little attention to the strongholds of modern Leningrad, the heavy industrial complexes, favouring those places that served consumer interests and the drive for industrial modernization. They visited the "Bolshevichka" clothing association and the "Svetlana" electronic appliance works. "All Leningrad products should be of world-market standard — no less!" demanded the General Secretary in the Smolny Institute, as if to assert that he was a prisoner neither of the Caucasus nor of Muscovite perspectives on the world, and that the Soviet Union was ready, under his leadership, to embrace again those European traditions for which Leningrad once stood.

Whatever his long-term aims, however, his short-term objective was unmistakable. He wanted to seize control of the stronghold of his long-standing rival, Grigori Romanov. The way in which he achieved his aim emphasised the differences between himself and his predecessors, from Khrushchev to Chernenko.

Romanov, 62, had until June 1983 been the city's feared and successful chief. With his elevation to the Central Committee as Secretary for Defence Industry, he became Gorbachev's main rival in the Politburo, with a formidable power-base in his home city. As Leningrad Party chief for almost 13 years — a longer run than all his communist

predecessors — Romanov had driven Leningrad's economy
forward fast. However, his industrial policies — unlike
Gorbachev's — were never marked by any particular concern for the social conditions of the population. And
Leningrad's apparently impressive achievements were
misleading. By far the major part of investment was in
heavy and defence industries. Basic research was neglected; light industries — such as textiles — were developing only sluggishly. In Leningrad, Romanov had created a
centralist model of apparent efficiency, attractive to those
elements of the Soviet elite whose aims were to achieve
modernization without administrative reforms and with
heavy industry as the engine of economic development.
That success underpinned his career, but it was not, in
Gorbachev's opinion, a model for the restructuring of the
Soviet economy.

Romanov's authority also had a political dimension.
Romanov was among the most extreme members of the Old
Guard. In Leningrad, he had battled against all contacts
with the West as well as any form of criticism of the
system. Human rights activists, who lived unmolested in
Moscow, were often arrested during visits to the Leningrad
area. He was a committed hawk and friend of the Military.
He had little time for Americans, and even less for Germans (understandable enough, perhaps — as a young soldier, he was among the defenders of Leningrad against the
murderous blockade by the German Wehrmacht and was
decorated for gallantry). Foreign visitors found him
aggressive and insecure when discussing external affairs.
Inspiration and improvisation were not his strong points.
He usually stuck rigidly to his notes. Moving to Moscow in
1983 as Central Committee Secretary, he opposed efforts to
achieve political detente with the West as a means of
lightening the economic burdens of Soviet military
spending.

In private life, Romanov, the son of a Novgorod farmer,
developed grandiose, almost tsarist pretensions. Towards
the end of Brezhnev's rule — but before Brezhnev's own
clan was pilloried for corruption — scandal spread about

the arrogant man with the steely blue eyes and boyish complexion. The most dramatic story to make the rounds involved his daughter's wedding feast. Romanov, it was said, demanded the dinner service of Catherine the Great — hundreds of unique and costly pieces — from the Hermitage, Leningrad's great museum. During the wedding breakfast, over-exuberant guests smashed a number of irreplacable glasses. Whether the rumours were true or not, Romanov became a target of attack for being arrogant and for indulging in unworthy behaviour in his private life.

On the night of Chernenko's death on March 10 1985, acting on the principle that attack was the best form of defence, Romanov suggested that Viktor Grishin be elected as the new General Secretary. That was the beginning of the end for him. Shortly thereafter he was compelled to give up his duties on the Central Committee to Yegor Ligachev, who later emerged as the second most powerful man in the Party.

Romanov's excessive drinking provided the reason for his dismissal. At the Hungarian Party Congress at the end of March 1985, he appeared drunk before the television cameras. On July 1 1985 he was retired by the Central Committee Plenum "for reasons of health" — six weeks after Gorbachev's Smolny Institute performance in Leningrad.

Gorbachev's dramatic speech on May 17 1985 and the undermining of Romanov were of course only a part of a wider campaign to win hearts and minds. From the start, Gorbachev showed a public dynamism uncharacteristic of Soviet leaders. But his efforts were more than public relations exercises. He planned them for political advantage to outflank and undermine his opponents. An early target was Viktor Grishin, the Moscow Party leader. Gorbachev was determined subtly but publicly to demonstrate how Grishin, one of Brezhnev's long-standing aides, had neglected the social needs of the Soviet capital. He announced he would visit a certain hospital, but then surprised his aides by going to a different one. There Gorbachev — well-informed by his daughter Irina, herself a medic married to a surgeon — asked a nurse about her earnings. 110 roubles per month, she replied, relatively high for this poorly paid profession.

"Is that enough?" asked Gorbachev.

"Of course not," answered the nurse.

"But she could put in overtime," interjected Grishin, weakly.

Gorbachev turned to a doctor, and asked, "Is the canteen food good?"

"How can it be at a price of 41 kopecks?" he answered.

By the end of the year, Gorbachev had achieved his aim. Grishin was pensioned off in December 1985.

As with his predecessors, when Gorbachev appeared in factories, the audience was selected by KGB and management. Now however the organizers were expected to present not mere prepared yes-men, but ordinary consumers ready to voice their complaints. "We'll talk quite openly here, otherwise there is no point in even starting," Gorbachev told the workers of Moscow's ZIL car works. They took him at his word, and showed him a thick file about their disagreements with ministerial planners.

On his walkabouts in Moscow supermarkets and on Leningrad's Nevsky Prospekt, he asked people what they wanted from Party and government. As in the West, such exchanges produced nothing more than commonplace responses. Nevertheless, the fact that these exchanges existed was electrifying. Whenever before could the citizens of Russia recall their leader behaving so uninhibitedly?

But shows of concern were not enough in themselves to initiate reform. There was a core of opposition from within the Party, or to be more precise from those whom Lenin called "the worst enemies — the communists who have learned not to battle against a bureaucracy but rather prefer to cover it up." Among these were not only Gorbachev's direct opponents, but also all those proponents of unyielding Party omnipotence. What was to become of the Party, they worried, if the people were to be consulted? Did

not Lenin himself deny a place to populist elements? Enthusiasm could lead to disappointed hopes. To encourage
the masses in this manner would bring only chaos and
anarchy. Thus all the old fears of the tsarist autocracy
were becoming resurrected among the Soviet bureaucracy.

That Gorbachev's brisk disposal of the rituals was suspect to many officials was clear from media reports. His
populist appeals and direct approaches to the people were
neutralized and weakened by the media. Even the KGB —
which Gorbachev had inherited as a fiefdom from Andropov and whose current director Viktor Chebrikov is one of
the keenest exponents of the new way — seemed uncertain
about Gorbachev's course. "Some people there ask: where
is all this leading to? Others declare: there is no alternative," I was told by a senior Party member with connec-
tions with the KGB.

Early on, Gorbachev himself gave an answer to the
objections of all those who wanted to curb his pace. In the
Ukrainian industrial centre Dnepropetrovsk, the former
stronghold of the Brezhnev clan, he told workers of the G.I.
Petrovsky metallurgy works at the end of June 1985: "The
question can arise: are we proceeding too drastically? No,
and we have not even once discussed this question in the
Central Committee of the CPSU. A different, that is to say
a more moderate approach, is not acceptable to us. The
times demand that we act in this way and in no other."

If his populism and charisma were a threat, so was the
breakneck speed with which Gorbachev placed his one-
man show above the principles of collective leadership. The
Old Guard favoured, and still favours, the principle of a
personality cult — but of a personality cult based on weakness of leadership, in which the elite participates as an
ordered hierarchy with clearly defined privileges. Brezhnev and Chernenko had tended this cult with their endless
presentations of honours, the larger-than-life portraits of
all leading politicians, and ritual quotations from the
General Secretary in every official speech. Gorbachev's
evolving form of personality cult promised a more activist

leader concerned with the substance of issues rather than with the rituals of leadership.

Immediately after Gorbachev's accession, the media were given firm instructions that it was no longer necessary or desirable to grace every leading article with a quotation by the Party leader. In Moscow, an anecdote went the rounds that was indicative of Gorbachev's new image. At *Pravda*, editor-in-chief Viktor Afanasyev's phone rings. It is Gorbachev. "Viktor Grigorievich," he asks, "Do you have the works of Lenin in your office?"

"Of course."

"Then be good enough to quote him in future — and not me."

This anecdote, though never more than Moscow's informal gossip, was of some significance. It exemplified what most threatened the Old Guard. Here was someone who did not just rely on the bureaucracy and collectively sanctioned empty phrases, but rather on himself, and his personal strength. Gorbachev's capacity to communicate, his charm, his ability to improvise, his quick reactions, his readiness to talk, his lordly gestures and attitudes appealed to the longing that many Soviet citizens have for a strong, "tsar-like" leader. But they were anathema to the privileged elite of the country's grey and plodding bureaucracy.

Herein lie dangers. Failure in the struggle with bureaucracy could lead Gorbachev to give vent to his arrogance or, on the other hand, force him to compromise. He could then suffer a loss of authority if the population demands that its raised expectations be fulfilled. And in a society unused to personal contact with its leadership, it is possible that familiarity will anyway breed contempt.

Only time will tell where all this will lead. As a communicator, perhaps Gorbachev's greatest challenge is to make the relationship between himself and the Soviet people two-way. He has a long way to go. At present, he expects more from the people than they expect from him. Those who have experienced him directly have been overwhelmed. But among the Soviet public hope and curiosity are usually laced with scepticism. "He's just a godfather, with his own mafia," a leading artist says. A female engineer told me: "In the last 20 years we have turned into something between Gogol and Orwell — an animal farm of dead souls. Now along comes a living soul. Will everyone wake up? I catch myself hoping, like an invalid who can suddenly walk 10 metres. But I just can't believe it yet." And a student from the Caucasus, Gorbachev's own region, summed up a common response: "Gorbachev can develop the charisma of a strong man. But how is he to become the bearer of our hopes? We just don't have that abstract hope for a general improvement in the situation in the way that you do. People just live their private lives in the circle of their friends. The leadership does not belong to us and has nothing to do with us. Well, that may have changed very slightly now. But so far as the man in the street is concerned, he says there won't be any changes in our generation, nor in the next, nor in the one after that."

The Campaigns Against Alcohol and Corruption

If Gorbachev's political style revealed latent conflicts within the Soviet Union, so too did his campaign against alcohol, for the "worst enemy" of present-day Soviet society is also the best of traditional friends. The campaign against alcohol thus has a symbolic significance. In tackling an evil so rooted in Soviet society — indeed in pre-Revolutionary Russia — Gorbachev's actions seem like a prologue to those greater, as yet unknown, actions by means of which he seeks to lead Soviet society out of its self-destructive lethargy.

Gorbachev and Yegor Ligachev were already making firm preparations for their campaign in the second half of 1984 while Chernenko was still in power. One month after Gorbachev's accession, at the beginning of April 1985, the Politburo voted for measures against drunkenness. It was clear from the start that this decision was directly connected with the planned structural improvements of the Soviet economy. *Kommunist* (No. 12/1985), the ideological organ of the Central Committee, even claimed that the attempts at modernization were dependent on the success of the campaign against alcohol.

The new leadership marched into the campaign with its ideological banners flying, thereby demonstrating its optimism at its ability to inspire the Party to a new commitment. The ideological significance of this campaign is clear from the slogan "For a sober leadership and a sober population," which Yegor Ligachev and KGB boss Viktor Chebrikov (among others) have used, the latter in his address on the 68th anniversary of the Revolution on November 6 1985.

And finally the campaign against alcohol was also intended as a tactical move. It was impossible to change everything at once. The imposition of sobriety seemed the simplest and most spectacular way to begin reform. It did not threaten political and social organizations, and it would be supported by Soviet women. (The extent to which the campaign was aimed at the approval of women was clear from readers' letters and commentaries in the press. For example, *Komsomolskaya Pravda* commented that mothers whose sons became alcoholics must find the experience even "worse than the war.")

The campaign started forcefully two months after Gorbachev assumed power. In three connected decisions that were published on May 17 1985, Party, government and Presidium announced a catalogue of measures and sanctions against alcohol. It was clear that the new orders were only the first steps, for the Central Committee simultaneously told a whole row of state committees, academies and ministries to compile an "all-state complex programme for the prevention and defeat of drunkenness and alcoholism."

Measures were to include: the removal of all officials who took part in or permitted drinking bouts; a ban on alcohol in work-places, official banquets and receptions, in sanatoria and tourist enterprises, on works outings and in all forms of public transport; the restriction of alcohol sales to the hours of 14.00–19.00; and the raising of the legal age for the purchase of alcohol from 18 to 21.

In addition, amongst other measures, the government issued detailed instructions for overcoming the "causes and conditions" of alcoholism. The State Committee for publishing was to produce more and better information on the subject. The Councils of Ministers in the republics were to spend up to three percent of the income of the housing administration on sports facilities. Wages and salaries of workers prone to alcohol abuse were to be transferred to savings bank accounts. The sale of tools, spare parts and hobby materials was to be considerably extended. And the sale of alcohol was to be prohibited in the vicinity of factories, construction sites, educational establishments, hospitals, railway stations, airports, cultural establishments and parks. The Presidium of the Supreme Soviet announced new penalties for alcohol abuse. And in September 1985, the price of vodka and brandy was increased by 30 percent, and that of sparkling wine by 15 percent. An unskilled worker now had to spend roughly one tenth of his monthly average pay for a litre of the cheapest vodka.

Price rises, the announcement of penalties, measures for re-education — nothing in all this was new. Gorbachev's predecessors had tried to enforce similar measures, until they ran out of steam. But Gorbachev's messianic enthusiasm for his version of the campaign was quite new. Like the battle against corruption, its effects went right to the top. Suddenly all were equal before the "dry law." At Soviet receptions, proletarians and parliamentarians of all nations found themselves united by fruit juice and mineral water. Vodka, brandy and for a time even wine and beer vanished from the buffets and canteens of car factories, academies, textile works and theatres. Foreign embassies were notified that they should take stricter measures to prevent their diplomats from drinking and driving.

This anti-alcoholic fervour had some odd effects. In summer 1985 in Moscow, I visited the exhibition of a talented artist from Gorbachev's northern Caucasus homeland. The items on show were neither modern nor "decadent": landscapes and village scenes of a lightly allegorical character. Nevertheless, just before the exhibition opened, 15 pictures had to be removed because, amongst other things, they also showed drunken peasants.

During those early weeks of the anti-alcohol campaign, television films were purged of alcohol by the censor. A key scene was cut out of the series "Mother Has Married Again" because the son and the new stepfather tried to ease the tension of their first meeting with a drink.

In mid-June 1985, Soviet television used its main evening news broadcast to pillory a small collection of rather sorry-looking alcoholics, showing the deliberation of a works court and the embarrassed delinquents in close-up. During this period, there were also many stories of draconian penalties. In one, an officer promoted to the rank of general celebrated the occasion with a meal in a restaurant, provided his guests with rather too much alcohol — and was retired on the spot. One anecdote concerned Gorbachev himself. When on an inspection trip that June, he visited a military hospital in Sebastopol, discovered that many of the high-ranking officers were being treated for severe alcoholism, and ordered them to be pensioned-off immediately.

Whether true or not, these stories show how unremitting was the drive and how widespread was the belief that the campaign against alcohol applied to the upper echelons, as well as to the rest of society. Drunks, who previously had been as much part of the Soviet street scene as the countless Militia men, were now rarely to be found. The number of crimes, misdemeanours and brawls committed by drunks declined. A representative of the Supreme Court announced at the end of November that between July and October 1985 the number of serious crimes went down by 10 percent.

But Gorbachev had not only taken on those who were directly or materially dependent on alcohol. He had also declared war on an attitude and a tradition. Two Russian traits were here in collision: the old conviction that everything evil, regressive and damaging could be excised if the axe were wielded with sufficient determination, and on the other hand the persistent feeling which, in Shakespeare's words,

"Makes us rather bear those ills we have
Than fly to others that we know not of."

Despite all the statistics, alcohol is for most Russians a perfectly bearable ill. Drinking is evidence of manly strength and the very essence of domestic hospitality. And drunkenness is, as ever, a covert appeal for sympathy. "In celebration, he drank until, raving and replete, he went back to the barracks," wrote Dostoevsky in *The House of the Dead*. "Now swaying and stumbling, to show them all that he was drunk, that he could 'carry it off,' and to gain general respect. Among Russian people one always finds a certain sympathy for drunks."

It was at just this sort of "sympathy" that Gorbachev's campaign was aimed. But though he could drum up considerable support, especially among women, he could not win the battle on the first attempt. In face of grumbling from the state retail, catering and entertainment concerns, he was forced to compromise. In Moscow 400 "places of alcohol" have since been reopened. Alcohol, other than as spirits, is once again relatively easy to buy. Major-General of the Militia Anatoli Zhorich announced that it was nonsense to say that the police had to "meet a quota" in arresting drunks. Though the highest representatives of the State and the Party continued to entertain with water and fruit juice, the strict regulations on the sale of alcohol were loosened. In accordance with good Leninist practice, Gorbachev made a tactical withdrawal without abandoning his long-term aim.

No such compromises have been made in his campaign against corruption, for after his accession it served him as a weapon to achieve three strategic objectives: to cut out as much of the dead wood as possible before the 27th Party Congress at the end of February 1986; to force the quickest possible change of generations at local and regional level; and to transform a society ruled by privilege into a society of achievers.

The first few months of the campaign against corruption led to a whole wave of reshuffles and to some draconian penalties. The two former high-ranking assistants of the Soviet State Committee for External Economic Relations, Smelyakov and Pavlov, who had been sentenced to death under Andropov, were executed. It now appeared that when working for the Technopromexport organization, Smelyakov, as president, and Pavlov, as leader of an overseas office, had accepted more than 200,000 roubles in bribes between 1977 and 1982 "in Moscow and abroad."

The anti-corruption drive also featured another first for the Gorbachev era — the involvement of the public in the campaign. On March 22 1985, a questionnaire appeared as a supplement in the Georgian Party newspaper *Zarya Vostoka*, in which readers were asked for information and opinions about corruption. Never before in the Soviet Union had there been such a wide-ranging public opinion survey as this.

The first item in the questionnaire was: which manifestations of the "property-owning mentality" — a euphemism for "corruption" — harmed personal interests the most? Nineteen possible answers were on offer, among them: theft of state property; abuse of official positions; swindling; bribery; and speculation with consumer goods and food.

Other questions aimed at assessing the level of tolerance for corruption and at discovering those areas of the economy in which, in the public's view, the battle against corruption should be increased. The questionnaire offered choices of measures to combat corruption, and asked where the respondents had gained their knowledge about corruption — from the media, conversations with family and friends, personal observation, rumour, official meetings, study at Marxist—Leninist institutes, propaganda lectures, public speeches by Soviet leaders, or conversations with superiors. At the end of the questionnaire, respondents were requested to put forward their own suggestions for a stronger campaign against corruption in Georgia.

The results of the survey have not been published, but the existence of the questionnaire is evidence of a new determination to consult the people.

Gorbachev, the Autocrat

In his first year in office, Gorbachev demonstrated an astonishing will to rule. Many had believed he possessed such a will, but few thought he could apply it with such vigour and speed. His rapid, relatively smooth progress to sole power is unprecedented in Soviet history, and his self-assurance more impressive to many Western observers than his charm. Some Western observers, particularly in West Germany, found the growth of his power and his aggressive approach unnerving. Was Gorbachev another Stalin? After all, Stalin was charming, at first. He too came from the Caucasus. Perhaps, like him, Gorbachev had his eye on unchallenged authority.

To some it seemed significant that there were subtle changes of attitude towards Stalin in the media. He was appearing again in Soviet documentary films. He was being mentioned in celebratory speeches. Stalin's former Foreign Minister, Vyacheslav Molotov, was readmitted into the Party at the age of 95. An obituary rehabilitated the dictator's last Security chief S.D. Ignatiev. The 100th anniversary of the birthday of Stalin's Senior Prosecutor, Nikolai Krylenko, was remembered, while the 50th anniversary of the death of Sergei Kirov, the popular Leningrad leader murdered on Stalin's orders on December 1 1934, went unremarked.

In fact, this re-emergence of Stalin, justified as an attempt to express a more realistic view of history, had started before Gorbachev's accession. And there is evidence that the gradual rehabilitation of Stalin has slowed since Chernenko's death.

Gorbachev did explicitly name Stalin in his May 1985 speech commemorating the 40th anniversary of the end of the war. Indeed, speaking as he was to war veterans for whom Stalin remained the war-time saviour of his country, he could hardly avoid doing so. But he mentioned his name only once, without praise, and with demonstrative difficulty. "The monumental efforts at the front and in the rear were led by the Party, its Central Committee and the State Defence Committee under the leadership of the General Secretary of the Central Committee of the CPSU(B), Josef Vissarionovich Stalin." As he said "Vissarionovich Stalin," Gorbachev stuttered. At the mention of Stalin's name the audience of veterans broke into applause. Normally, Gorbachev would have followed the Kremlin custom of joining in the applause. But this time he remained studiedly motionless, and then continued his speech without even waiting for the applause to end. He could not have demonstrated his reluctance to mention Stalin's name more clearly.

Some have nevertheless seen a similarity between Stalin's "socialism in one country" and Gorbachev's insistence on economic not military strength as a guarantee of national security. But there is no real comparison. Stalin sacrificed millions to heavy industry without the slightest consideration for the population. Gorbachev, on the other hand, strives to give priority to light and consumer goods industries as the prime movers for economic effectiveness. He makes no secret of the fact that he is not acting solely from humanitarian concern. He wants to keep the Soviet Union as powerful as possible and for that reason he insists on iron discipline. There is a clear difference, however, between the young Stalin's dark and introverted obsessions and Gorbachev's urging for more political openness.

In any event, Stalin is not the only one to regain some standing under Gorbachev. It is significant, although hardly noticed in the West, that the new leadership set the opening of the 27th Party Congress for February 25 1986, the 30th anniversary of Khrushchev's secret address about Stalin's crimes. During the summer of 1985, a television documentary about the 1957 Moscow Festival of Youth showed a good-humoured Khrushchev in the Lenin stadium, with a dove of peace in his hand. It was the first time since his fall in 1964 that Khrushchev had been shown on Soviet screens as Party chief. In the coded language of Soviet officialdom, this choice of date was clearly intended as an attempt to give Khrushchev as well as Stalin a more appropriate niche in Soviet history.

In assessing Gorbachev's attitude towards Stalin, Khrushchev and towards recent history, his posture towards the Russites, the nationalist wing of the Moscow intelligentsia, has scarcely been noticed in the West.

One of his closest advisors, Alexander Yakovlev, head of the propaganda department of the Central Committee and a prominent member of Gorbachev's entourage at the Geneva summit, is an openly declared opponent of Russite nationalism.

Gorbachev, too, has declared himself against the nationalists, but in less overt ways. One particular incident, involving the Moscow Artists' Theatre (MKhAT), is indicative as much of the style as the substance of Gorbachev's leadership. The theatre is known for its association with the work of Stanislavsky, Meyerhold, Chekhov and others of the tradition that looks on Russia as part of the West. The Russites had criticized the theatre for its performances of plays by a number of Jewish writers. Antisemitic rumours began to make the rounds, together with assertions that the theatre was no longer as good as it used to be. Thereupon on May 1 1985 Gorbachev and his wife appeared in the theatre to watch Chekhov's *Uncle Vanya*, which he had chosen to see against the specific advice of the Ministry of Culture.

After his visit, Gorbachev called up theatre director Oleg Yefremov, congratulated him, praised specific actors, and finally declared: "I know that you have had a few unpleasantnesses. Please do carry on without worrying about the future." Yefremov answered that he would like to discuss the theatre more with the Party leader, to which Gorbachev replied: "First, I have to set the wheels in motion. Then I will gladly have a discussion with you," adding: "I need the support of the intelligentsia." Finally, he inquired if he could do anything practical for the theatre in the short term. Yefremov pointed out to him that their old building in the centre of Moscow had long been in the process of reconstruction, and that there were insufficient resources available for this. Gorbachev indicated that something could be done. A few days later a small announcement appeared in the evening paper *Vechernyaya Moskva* that grants were being made available for the historic Moscow Artists' Theatre building — a small but clear indication that Gorbachev's autocratic methods are not comparable to Stalin's.

Gorbachev's Men

On April 22 1985, the 115th anniversary of Lenin's birth, the Politburo Members who in the previous month had voted for Gorbachev and against Grishin celebrated together, taking their places in the Kremlin's Congress Palace according to a carefully arranged hierarchical order. But by the next day, this old hierarchy was gone, upset by the addition of three men who had not previously been in the Politburo; indeed, two of them — Yegor Ligachev, who was simultaneously promoted to No. 2 in the Party and chief ideologist, and Nikolai Ryzhkov, the new economic manager and now Prime Minister — had not even been Candidate Members. The third, Viktor Chebrikov, Director of the KGB, had become a Candidate Member not long before. Since then, these men, together with Gorbachev, have formed the inner leadership in the Kremlin, the vanguard of the army of new administrators who are to put Gorbachev's ideas into effect.

Together, these three correspond to the three basic patterns which define Gorbachev's followers: the dynamic, hard-working, committed Party organizer, who fights bureaucracy but still believes fully in control and the viability of the system (Yegor Ligachev); the competent specialist, whose career is outside the Party machine (Nikolai Ryzhkov); and finally the convert, who follows Gorbachev's path because it is expedient to do so (Viktor Chebrikov). (For more details, see Appendix 2.)

On the same day that clarified the status of the top three, a further change in the hierarchical order was confirmed. The KGB ranked before the Army. Defence Minister Sergei Sokolov, previously simply a member of the Central Committee, was promoted, but only to be a Candidate Member of the Politburo. The post of Central Committee Secretary for Agriculture, which had been Gorbachev's springboard to power, was given to Viktor Nikonov.

The next big change came nine weeks later, on July 1. A further plenum sent Gorbachev's rival, Grigori Romanov, until then Politburo Member and Central Committee Secretary for Heavy and Defence Industries, into retirement without a word of appreciation for his services. One of Gorbachev's confidants from his Komsomol days in the Caucasus, Eduard Shevardnadze, previously Party leader of Georgia and Candidate Member of the Politburo, was promoted to full Member. Boris Yeltsin became Central Committee Secretary for Construction, and Lev Zaikov Central Committee Secretary for Heavy and Defence Industries. The next day, July 2, the 28-year career of the world's longest-serving Foreign Minister came to an end, when Andrei Gromyko was given the symbolic post of President. Shevardnadze became the new Foreign Minister (a change described in greater detail in the next chapter).

Twelve weeks later, on September 27, Prime Minister Nikolai Tikhonov also retired. The 80-year-old head of government, a loyal friend of Brezhnev and Chernenko, and who for that reason had been among Gorbachev's opponents, wrote a valedictory message to the Secretary General, which Gromyko read before the Supreme Soviet: "My dear Mikhail Sergeievich! Recently my health has been noticeably deteriorating. The Medical Council has been pressing explicitly for the cessation of my active duties and consequently for my retirement. As hard as it is for me to direct this plea to you, I am nevertheless forced to request that you, Mikhail Sergeievich, and the Politburo Central Committee, should retire me for reasons of health. I am boundlessly grateful to our dear Communist Party for everything that it has done for me. I particularly want to mention the friendly, comradely atmosphere that has been created in the Politburo in recent times. I only wish I could go on working and working with you."

Only that summer, Tikhonov had had his draft Five-Year Plan sent back brusquely by Gorbachev for reworking. His submissive letter helped to ensure that he (unlike Romanov) at least received the thanks of the Supreme Soviet for his "considerable contribution to the economic, social and cultural development of the country." Nikolai Ryzhkov, a quarter-century younger, became the new Prime Minister.

Two and a half weeks later, on October 14, Gorbachev removed the greatest obstacle to his plans of modernization: the Chairman of the State Planning Commission, Nikolai Baybakov, was pensioned off after 20 years in office. Whereas Baybakov had only been Deputy Prime Minister, his successor, Nikolai Talyzin, took on the office of First Deputy Chairman of the Council of Ministers and on October 15 also became a Candidate Member of the Politburo. Yegor Ligachev who left as the only man in the powerful double position of Politburo Member and Central Committee Secretary, aside from Gorbachev himself.

What did it all mean? There are three aspects which appear remarkable. Firstly, Gorbachev has confirmed his tendency to surround himself with regional Party secretaries. Secondly, it has become clear that the new open style, in particular the campaign against corruption, will not make rapid, fundamental changes to either political culture or Party structure. The reason is simple: lack of protection in the lower strata of the Party for those who criticize. Thirdly, for this reason Gorbachev has led from the front by himself encouraging independent criticism in the media. This aspect of his style of government has reinforced the other sweeping changes in personnel.

In summer 1985, for instance, *Sovietskaya Rossiya*, the government newspaper of the Russian Republic (under its Prime Minister, Andropov's "Mr. Clean" and Gorbachev's ally Vitali Vorotnikov) attacked the 77-year-old Mayor of Moscow, Vladimir Promyslov. The newspaper's special correspondent reported in detail about planning fraud in Moscow's construction industry. And he did it in a style which no Soviet journalist would dare to use, even under Gorbachev, if he had not had approval from the highest levels. The more the "rubbish in the house" was piling up, the article stated, the worse it was for the "authority of the owner." Everybody knew that this attack on the frequently criticized mayor was aimed at Moscow's Party leader, Viktor Grishin.

And indeed, shortly thereafter, this member of the most powerful body in the Soviet leadership had to admit in a letter to the very same paper that its criticism had been justified. Without signing himself as a Politburo Member, Grishin confirmed the "serious shortcomings" in Moscow's housing construction, for which the responsible workers had received punishment through the Party and the administration. Grishin was ousted at the end of 1985 and Promyslov was pensioned off in early 1986.

Gorbachev encouraged further criticism against the 73-year-old former Brezhnev intimate Dinmukhamed Kunayev, Member of the Politburo and Party boss of Kazakhstan. This time the attack was aimed at the local Party chief through the Party leader of the industrial Chimkent Region, Asanbai Askarov. According to official reports, Askarov had tolerated financial irregularities, including the falsification of planning figures. Under the heading "Suiting Style and Methods of Work to the Level of New Tasks," the Kazakh newsagency KazTAG reported on the Plenum of the Chimkent Regional Committee on July 12, mentioning a number of faults in the district: faltering enterprises, low work productivity, poor use of industrial potential, faulty houses, the diversion of energy and resources, low harvests, the falsification of plans, and speculation. Consequently, the Plenum had removed Askarov. It was already clear that Kunayev was to be next.

In his first seven months Gorbachev achieved more than most of his predecessors achieved in seven years. With his new engineers (Ligachev, Ryzhkov, Chebrikov, Yeltsin, Zaikov and Talyzin were all trained engineers), Gorbachev, lawyer and agronomist, had a team which (at least initially) appeared more solid than any Kremlin leadership since the death of Stalin. (Appendix 2 provides sketches of some of the more significant men chosen by Gorbachev.)

In parallel with the changes at the top, there was a wave of reshuffles throughout the country, aiming to change generations at local and regional level, and to bring as many allies as possible into the new 300-strong Central Committee, to be elected at the 27th Party Congress in early 1986. Before the end of 1985, changes involved 14 ministers at national level, 25 regional Party chiefs and eight departmental heads of the Central Committee in Moscow.

Gorbachev's "Reconstruction"

What is behind all the changes in personnel and structure? Published documents and measures taken reveal evidence of considerable change (though it was far from the Party throwing "its doors and windows wide open for anything progressive," as Gorbachev promised in December 1984). At the beginning of November 1985, Soviet newspapers published the draft of a new Party statute, which was to be ratified by the 27th Party Congress in February 1986. The statute allows for a remarkable innovation, which is important for the encouragement of intra-Party discussion and criticism: "A Party Member has the right... to criticize at Party meetings, at Party conferences and Party Congresses as well as in plenary sessions of committees, any Party institution he wishes, and any communist he wishes without regard for his position." In short, any Party institution may be criticized, not only individuals.

This was an acknowledgement of past failures. Under Stalin, the Security Service held power over the Party, and made arrests without regard for the Party rulebook. Khrushchev therefore ensured that the Party provided immunity from KGB intrusions into the upper echelons of the Party. Anyone who broke the law had first to be expelled from the Party before he could be brought before the

Courts. But under Brezhnev, this immunity increasingly
served to shield corrupt Party Members. The new statute
states, "Individuals who are found guilty of punishable
offences will be expelled from the ranks of the Party." In
other words, the law comes first. The Courts need no longer
wait on the Party.

On October 26 1985 the Soviet newspapers published the
draft of the Party programme, which was also to be ratified
at the 27th Party Congress. This document is a reworked
edition of the programme that Khrushchev designed in
1961, according to which the Soviet Union was already to
have overtaken the West in per-capita production by 1981.

The new Party programme was ordered for the 27th
Congress by Brezhnev back in 1981. It therefore came two
or three years too early to bear Gorbachev's stamp outright. Some of the old spirit remains. The Americans, for
instance, are declared to be the greatest threat to peace:
"The main bastion of international reaction is the imperialism of the USA. It is from this, above all, that the
threat of war emanates."

But the Party no longer sees "the fatal inevitability of a
world war." And in contrast to Khrushchev's old programme, the new version underlines that in a global military
conflict "there would be neither victors nor vanquished."
Peaceful co-existence is no longer described as a "specific
form of class warfare" with undiminished "ideological"
conflict. And Brezhnev too, whose rule the Soviet press
today circumscribes as a time of "toadyism and sycophan-
cy," comes in for criticism.

The new programme also does without any high-flown
comparisons with Western industrialized nations. The
higher standard of living which the Party promises to
Soviet citizens is not set out in facts and figures, which —
like Khrushchev's — could later make a grotesque and
embarrassing contrast to reality. The "dictatorship of the
proletariat," no longer seen as the indispensable prerequisite for the transition from capitalism to socialism, is
only mentioned in passing in a historical context. The
Soviet Union is no longer explicitly put forward as a model

for the whole world, or even for the socialist world.

But even those objectives which the Party does set itself are daunting. Without saying how the changes are to be achieved, the programme promises to boost work productivity "by a factor of 2.3–2.5 within the next 15 years" and to improve quality so that Soviet products "meet the highest technical, economic, aesthetic and other demands of consumers and are capable of competing in world markets."

The programme also has a whole new heading on "Social Politics." Here again we can see how the Party presses for greater productivity, not only through more discipline but also through incentives: "Social policy will have increasing influence on economic growth." The Party, says the programme, "will actively carry out *measures for the heightening of the role of the main links in the productive chain* [emphasis as in the original] — the associations and industrial concerns — and will consistently pursue the extension of their rights and economic independence, and the raising of their responsibility for and interest in good results." It is clear, then, that Gorbachev intends no mere placebo, but rather a radical treatment.

What treatment exactly? Mainly a continued assault on bureaucratic inefficiency. At a special conference on questions of scientific and technical progress on June 11 1985, Gorbachev declared: "We would be deluding ourselves, if we were to hope that the state planning commission of the USSR could co-ordinate all the links in the chain of relationships between the different branches of industry... the role and functions of ministries must change... the higher management in the different branches must be considerably reduced, and the rest must be completely dismembered."

This has led to the creation of new super-ministries for machine construction and agriculture, and to the sudden abolition of numerous administrative posts. Thus in the new State Committee for Agro-industry (Gosagroprom), which directs both the agricultural and the food industries, only some 4,000 people are now employed out of the total of six ministries that were integrated into this department. Of some 250 original branches in these ministries, only 25 were to remain at the end. By the end of 1985 more than 7,000 workers in this field alone were said to have been dismissed. Those who are fired generally receive 3–6 months' salary and are then given three alternatives: to accept the offer of a new post (with fewer or no privileges), to accept retraining, or to look for new work themselves.

Even while many employees of the agricultural administration were trying to arrange jobs in the new super-department, a further Central Committee resolution dissolved all superfluous branches of the Ministry for Machine Construction, cut back on jobs and ordered that future employees were to be selected on merit. Other ministries were subjected to a total recruitment ban.

These are radical changes. But how radical is "radical"? Does Gorbachev want to decentralize further? Or does he simply want to make the existing system work better? In June 1985, Gorbachev's No. 2, Ligachev, declared that the "revolutionary transformations" would take place without "deviations to a market economy and private enterprise." Was this the last word?

Certainly, the new generation of leaders can see the danger of change, for three main reasons.

Firstly, they have been moulded by a past in which hurried reforms, from Khrushchev to the Prague Spring, led inevitably to the loss of Party control. An awareness of this simple reality is an integral part of the political psychology of the new leadership.

Secondly, the promotion of private enterprise and entrepreneurial independence carries considerably greater political risks in a vast country with heterogeneous potential markets (from the Baltic to the Caucasus, from mercantile to bazaar traditions) than it does in a small homogeneous state like Hungary. If Russian hegemony of its multi-national, multi-ethnic and multi-cultural empire is to remain secure — an assumption with which no Kremlin leadership can afford to gamble — then all-out decentralization and a recourse to market economics is scarcely viable. Moscow, and particularly the European population of the Soviet Union, must continue to pay a high economic price for its political primacy.

Thirdly, the new leadership must acknowledge and bring into their calculations the strong reservations against "reconstruction" held by the bureaucracy, leaders in heavy industry and much of the Military. After all, the military–industrial complex is still by definition outside the reach of market forces.

Gorbachev is therefore bound to prefer a rationalized, centrally administered economy on the pattern of East Germany as opposed to the Hungarian model of expanded private initiative and industrial autonomy. His options are limited by the very size of the Soviet Union and its economic structure.

What of the future? Gorbachev has used his first year principally to create the foundation for change. He was able to achieve this faster than any Soviet Party leader before him. To that extent his fresh initiative has been a success. But, in the second phase, he must demonstrate that he can achieve some real breakthroughs.

For Gorbachev's honeymoon with the essentially conservative Soviet establishment can only have a limited life. During this period, the combination of declarations and tinkering with the administrative system will not have any fundamental effects on the foundations and workings of the Soviet economy. If growth rates continue to decline, so will Gorbachev's image. He will then face a decisive choice: to doctor the statistics and thus evade responsibility, or to institute reforms to make careful changes in the structure of the central planning system.

If he wants to avoid the first path and to follow the second, he will need to develop his contacts with the West. Are conditions in the world outside favourable enough to help him put his own house in order? This is the question addressed in the following chapter.

8

Gorbachev's "Window on the West"

It was 9.30 on Tuesday, July 2 1985. In the Kremlin, the 1,500 delegates of the Supreme Soviet were gathering for their summer session. The limousines of foreign ambassadors were being discreetly directed to a side-street in the interior courtyard. In the meeting hall of the large Kremlin Palace, Uzbek and Kirghiz women delegates with long pigtails under their brightly coloured headscarves crowded together in rows. Directly in front of them sat the Supreme Commander of the Warsaw Pact, Marshal Kulikov, greeting delegates with a fraternal kiss. Further back, a greying Marshal Ogarkov talked animatedly to the man in front of him, the Director of the American Institute, Georgi Arbatov.

Down in the hall, there seemed to be no hint of tension. But up in the narrow galleries and corridors, diplomats and journalists grew tenser by the minute. For days rumours had been circulating about whether Gorbachev or Gromyko would be elected as the new Head of State (or more precisely: Chairman of the Presidium of the Supreme Soviet). Since 1977, the roles of Party leader and Head of State had been combined. Surely, it was whispered, it would suit Gorbachev to preserve this tradition? Did not the fall of his rival, Grigori Romanov, the previous day prove that the new General Secretary was aiming at complete control?

At exactly 10.00 a.m. Gorbachev entered the hall to brief applause, but no ovation. Apparently, the Party leader sought no personal tributes. Only Prime Minister Tikhonov and Foreign Minister Gromyko took their seats next to the General Secretary, the two other chairs in the front row remaining empty. In the rows behind were the Politburo Members, no longer seated according to rank, but randomly, as though no longer needing to demonstrate their relative status.

Lev Tolkunov, the Chairman of the Union Council in the Supreme Soviet, and a Gorbachev supporter, opened the session. He spoke only a few sentences, announcing that the General Secretary would propose the motion for the election of the new Chairman of the Presidium of the Supreme Soviet. A murmur ran through the hall. Up in the gallery, a Yugoslav journalist sucked in his breath and muttered: "So it's not Gorbachev after all!"

Gorbachev stepped forward. Because the country was facing such momentous tasks, he said, the Plenum of the Central Committee has considered it advisable that the General Secretary should concentrate fully on the work of the Central Party organizations. For that reason he proposed that Andrei Andreievich Gromyko should be elected as Chairman of the Supreme Soviet. Gorbachev commended the new Head of State, though by Soviet standards by no means effusively, and ended with the proposal that Gromyko should be relieved of his duties as Foreign Minister and as First Deputy Prime Minister.

Many of the observers crammed together in the gallery gave a deep sigh, as though overwhelmed by the significance of the moment. What did it mean? Gromyko stripped of power? Or raised still higher? For the moment, no one knew.

Shortly after Gromyko's brief, unemotional acceptance, there occurred an event no one could have anticipated. The 80-year-old Prime Minister, Nikolai Tikhonov, stepped to the microphone and in a powerful, slightly hoarse voice

proposed as the new Foreign Minister Eduard Ambro-
sievich Shevardnadze, Party leader of the Caucasian republic of Georgia, and never previously involved in foreign
policy.

The first reaction on the upper floors of the Kremlin hall
was laughter, amazement and disbelief. Diplomats cupped
their ears, as if uncertain of what was being said. Many
appeared incapable of grasping what they had heard. A
provincial baron was to succeed the doyen of international
politics!

In fact, these surprising moves were brilliant, calculated
and far-sighted. Gorbachev had done something more subtle than ensure outright one-man rule. Firstly, the Foreign
Ministry was taken from the hands of a career diplomat
and returned to the direction of a Party man, a man with
the organizational talent to transform the foreign service
into Gorbachev's tool. Secondly, with Shevardnadze from
Georgia (along with Aliyev from Azerbaijan) another in-
digenous representative from Caucasia was brought into
the collective leadership. Thirdly, and most significantly,
by choosing a man without foreign experience, Gorbachev
announced his intention of taking responsibility for his
own foreign policy, of becoming a statesman.

The reconstruction of the Soviet economy could not be
effected in the isolation Gromyko had imposed. There had
to be a new way of dealing with America. Crises would
have to be avoided as much as possible and contacts increased, in order to gain time for modernization at home.
For this reason, in the short term at least, Gorbachev had
to shelve Gromyko's insistence that improvements in US–
Soviet relations be conditional on Washington's immediate
renunciation of the Star Wars programme. The Geneva
summit at the end of the year would set a seal on the new
approach.

In the following months, in order to establish this political strategy in ideological and propaganda terms, Gorbachev planted the idea of communal, global responsibility
for arms control (an extension of a regional policy that
some socialist countries, under the leadership of Janos

Kadar and Erich Honecker, had been trying to effect in 1983–4). How fully, and how long before his accession to power, Gorbachev had developed this concept cannot be said with certainty. What is certain is that in speeches and statements he never presented himself as a cold warrior or as a spokesman for increased armaments. Even while Gromyko was answering President Reagan's crusading anti-communism with blasts of cold war invective — in June 1984 — Gorbachev was already sounding more positive. At the same time, he focused less on the United States and more on the rest of the world. In the first statement that was given close attention in the West, he said on February 20 1985: "We accord great importance to the normalization of relations with the United States and to honest negotiation with them on all current problems of international life, but at the same time we do not forget for an instant that the world is not confined to this one country." The Old World, he said — "our common house" — must be protected from becoming a "testing ground for the Pentagon's doctrine of 'limited' nuclear war."

Shortly after coming to power, Gorbachev announced a moratorium on the deployment of Soviet medium-range missiles, to take effect initially until November 1985. This was significant as a gesture, but of no practical importance, for the Soviet Union had already deployed many more warheads — 1,242 in 414 SS-20 missiles — than NATO, which had deployed only 134 of the planned 527 single-warhead Pershing II and Cruise missiles.

Concurrent with this announcement, Gorbachev once again hinted that he had doubts about the bi-polar model of the world. "The relationships between the Soviet Union and the United States are an extremely important factor in international politics," he said, as published in *Pravda* on April 8 1985, "however we do not view the world solely through the prism of these relationships. We understand the importance of other countries." Many Western observers jumped to the conclusion that Gorbachev had no new ideas for a dialogue with the USA and that his only purpose was to drive a wedge between the Americans and the

Europeans. When he proposed a freeze of all weapons and developments to be negotiated in Geneva, his tactic was described by NATO officials in Brussels as a "classic example of Soviet diplomacy, which aims to split the Western Alliance."

On the other hand, Brezhnev and Andropov had failed to block the stationing of American missiles in Europe. Previous attempts to divide the Western Alliance had come to nothing, and Gorbachev would have drawn some lessons from these failures.

In fact, Gorbachev — advised amongst others by Yakovlev, who had been pointing out the increasing "polycentrism" in the world — was already starting to apply his new foreign policy. His first steps on the diplomatic stage following Chernenko's funeral — his wooing of China, India and Japan — made it clear that he was interested in more than driving a wedge between the Americans and the Europeans. In quick succession, he received Rajiv Gandhi (upgrading Asia and the non-aligned movement), American Trade Secretary Malcolm Baldridge (emphasising Soviet—American economic relations), West German SPD Chairman Willy Brandt (wooing peace movements and social democratic parties) and Italian Prime Minister Benito Craxi (asserting a readiness to improve relations between Comecon and the European Community).

All these pieces soon formed a pattern the outlines of which became increasingly clear over the next few months.

The Socialist Nations

To understand more precisely Gorbachev's policies towards his socialist allies demands a brief look back to the period before his accession, recalling in more detail some of the developments mentioned in previous chapters.

On October 24 1983, during Andropov's term, Tass put out a message with the curious heading "In the Defence Ministry of the USSR." It. was not from the Party, but rather from the Army, which assumed responsibility for announcing the start of additional Soviet measures against the planned deployment of American missiles in Western Europe. Preparations would commence, it said, for the deployment of missile complexes in East Germany and Czechoslovakia.

This announcement — almost a month before the Bonn government resolved to accept Pershing II and Cruise missiles — came as a surprise. But East Germany had moved even faster than the Soviet Military. Two days previously, the East German Party newspaper *Neues Deutschland* had published a letter to Erich Honecker from the Lutheran— Protestant Church community of Dresden-Loschwitz. This said: "We are filled with horror at the idea that when we are all condemning the deployment of nuclear missiles in Western Europe, we should at the same time be taking similar countermeasures on our own territory, and that we and our children will have to live in close proximity with nuclear missiles." The Church community, whose letter would not have been published if it had not coincided with the interests of the Party, appealed directly to Honecker: "We wish to encourage you and at the same time to implore you urgently, to continue and to expand the dialogue between the two German states, so that confidence may grow as a basis for a partnership of security, or to use your words, a coalition of common sense."

At the 7th Plenum of the East German Central Committee on November 25 1983, Honecker himself took on the role of European guardian of peace. Unmistakably, he signalled that he was distancing himself from Gromyko's intransigent policies. These measures, he said, were necessary to prevent the United States gaining military and strategic superiority, but they "will not gain acclamation in our country. We were never supporters of the arms race and we will never be so." And further: "It is of great importance to continue the political dialogue with all our power."

East Germany won support from Hungary, Romania, and even Bulgaria, Moscow's most loyal ally. A situation arose which had never before existed in the Warsaw Pact.

This was not one country drifting away from Soviet control, as had happened in several unrelated instances since 1945, but rather four states taking part together in a move towards a European "community of responsibility."

The split between the Soviet Union and its socialist allies was then raised to a new level in Moscow by the coalition of the Military, the Central Committee external departments and the Foreign Ministry, which urged a hard line. They let MiG jet fighters thunder over Berlin and had the propagandists of the Prague Party organ *Rude Pravo* direct the offensive. Loyal to Moscow, this newspaper attacked East Germany and Hungary, saying that every effort by a socialist country to gain unilateral advantages from the capitalist world damaged the prestige of socialism. Nor was it the task of small socialist countries to promote compromises between the superpowers.

But the dispute was not the result of wilfulness in the East European nations. The Kremlin itself had unwittingly provided the impetus for such opinions. The Soviet Union could offer its Comecon partners neither reserves nor reforms, neither aid in the current energy crisis nor viable recipes for the reduction of mounting debts. She had forced her allies into self-help. Now, none of the socialist countries could manage without the economies of Western Europe. The Eastern European leaders saw the economic links they had carefully constructed seriously threatened by the superpowers' confrontation.

Ironically, this was in accordance with Gorbachev's policy for his own country, though it was still opposed by the balance of power in the Kremlin leadership. Gorbachev was therefore eager not to leave Honecker out in the cold. At the beginning of August 1984, Lev Tolkunov, Chairman of the Union Council in the Supreme Soviet, formerly a confidant of Andropov and now a supporter of Gorbachev, wrote in *Sovietskaya Kultura* that there were possibilities "of achieving agreements and understandings between nations of differing social systems... the policies of detente by no means belong to the past."

With these words, a glimmer of light was seen to be

shining through a crack in the door which Foreign Minister Gromyko had slammed shut. Gorbachev took his opportunity. He was able to persuade both Erich Honecker (who
had been summoned to a secret meeting with the Kremlin
leaders on August 12 1984) and Todor Zhivkov to postpone
their proposed visits to Bonn. A direct clash between East
European interests and Gromyko's policy was thus
avoided, and time gained to work on a compromise.

Even after Gorbachev's accession to power, there were
still clear differences in Moscow on the issue of how to deal
with Eastern Europe. Gorbachev and his advisors urged
increased integration in Comecon, but were prepared to
allow the other states contacts with the West in their
attempts to solve their economic problems, and even some
limited cultural independence. On the other hand, the Party foreign policy experts demanded a strict control of all
states in the Warsaw Pact.

The climax to this grumbling dispute approached when,
on June 21 1985, a leading article appeared in *Pravda*
under the pseudonym "O. Vladimirov." In Moscow, it was
thought fairly certain that the pseudonym was that of a
Central Committee expert in Eastern Europe, Oleg Rakhmanin. Rakhmanin had long been seen as a supporter of an
orthodox line, who maintained close links with the ultra-
conservative Prague Party leadership. Essentially, "Vladimirov" warned that imperialism was attempting to ex-
aggerate the individuality of the socialist countries, to tear
them from the USSR and to "achieve an erosion or even a
transformation of their social orders." He spoke of "rus-
sophobia and anti-sovietism" and complained that "re-
visionist, nationalist and clerical [i.e. Church] interests"
had reached "the surface of ideological life." In the face of
such threats, the fraternal parties should show solidarity.

The *Pravda* article was quickly rebutted. In *Kommunist*,
the No. 2 man in the Hungarian Party leadership, Karoly
Nemeth, emphasised his country's independent line. The
private agricultural sector would continue to play an important part in Hungary, he wrote, and Budapest remained
determined to consolidate "the mutually advantageous

economic and scientific links with the developed capitalist states." In the same edition of *Kommunist* there was also an article by Oleg Bogomolov, the Director of the Moscow Institute for the Economics of the Socialist World System, who had already advised Andropov and who had for the first time used the word "reform," in *Pravda* in March 1983. Bogomolov stated: "The individual socialist states... are in differing phases of economic development. They have differing economic and political structures and traditions."

Such publicly expressed differences continued through 1985. In mid-December, *Pravda*, whose commentaries on questions of the socialist community continued to be influenced by Party conservatives, described the intervention of Soviet forces in Czechoslovakia as "aid... which resulted from the appeal by communists and true Czechoslovak patriots, and prevented a bloodbath, which the counter-revolution had prepared." Almost at the same time an unusual plea for equal rights for the socialist countries appeared in the magazine *Working Class and the World Today*, which is published by the Institute of the International Workers' Movement in the Academy of Sciences.

Overall, however, the dispute seems to have abated temporarily with a recognition of the individuality of socialist countries. Both the renewal of the Warsaw Pact in Warsaw in April 1985 and the Eastern bloc summit in Sofia on October 22–23 passed moderate communiques and declarations. And in their new Party programme, the Kremlin leadership asserts "all states, great and small, whatever their capacities, whatever their geographical situation, and whatever their social system, can and must take part in the defusing of conflict situations as well as in measures for the reduction of tensions and the containment of the arms race."

Asia, Afghanistan and Israel

Gorbachev began to adopt a more flexible policy towards the Middle East and Asia as soon as he came to power.

During Rajiv Gandhi's visit in May 1985, he brought up a long-forgotten idea, that of a collective Asian security system. He began to work for better relations with China and with Japan, which Gorbachev hopes will play an important part in the Soviet Union's modernization. In the Middle East, the Kremlin hinted it might accept Israel's right to exist and signalled a willingness to resume relations, which had been broken off in 1967. In return, Gorbachev would like a new Middle East conference, and so the return of the Soviet Union to a stage from which it was pushed by US Secretary of State Henry Kissinger in 1973.

Afghanistan remains a thorny problem. Gorbachev indicated he intended to withdraw Soviet troops — some 115,000 men — and at the Geneva summit in November 1985 the American delegation came away with the impression that he was more serious in his search for a way out than his predecessors. Immediately before the discussions between Reagan and Gorbachev, Soviet Central Committee member Nikolai Shishlin declared that the decision to send in the troops in December 1979 had been a "difficult decision in an emergency situation." Today the Soviet Union was "really not very happy" to have troops stationed in Afghanistan. It was working for their withdrawal with the "highest priority."

The words coming out of Moscow after Geneva seemed equally conciliatory. In an unusually open leading article in December 1985, on the 6th anniversary of the Soviet invasion, *Pravda* admitted for the first time that the "April revolution" was by no means accepted by all Afghans. Instead there continued to be resistance which could be traced back to "errors," which had been made particularly in the first phase of the revolution by the "enforcement of social reforms without regard for the actual situation as well as the social and national characteristics of the country." Most notably, *Pravda* said it was necessary "to create an atmosphere of positive dialogue between public and political forces, including those who had previously taken up hostile positions towards the revolution." *Pravda* even proposed the inclusion of private enterprise in a "national rebirth," an amazing statement since up to that point foreign interventions had supposedly been exclusively responsible for the poor state of affairs in Afghanistan.

Gorbachev is in a delicate position. If he is too ready to compromise on Afghanistan, he could gain a reputation for weakness as the man who put the seal on a Soviet defeat. But if he insists on continuing the vicious occupation, he risks losing his image as a rational reformer.

Gorbachev and Europe

Gorbachev's flexibility is not just a diplomatic ploy. It governs his behaviour, as he demonstrated on his visit to France in October 1985, after a speech by the Mayor of Paris, Jacques Chirac, in the City Hall.

Chirac's speech went on far beyond the matter in hand. In schoolmasterly fashion, he gave his guest a global political report. Gorbachev, sitting on a red-upholstered throne surrounded by tapestries, chandeliers, stucco and mirrors, nodded politely. But then, when the Russian translation was read out, the warm expression gradually froze on Gorbachev's face. He threw back his head with a slight jerk and pushed his lower lip and chin forward, an expression he adopts when preparing for a counter-attack. For Chirac, who was also leader of the Gaullist RPR, had spoken out against the Soviet Union's record on the rule of law and human rights. "The nobler our hopes," he said, "the more bitter are our disappointments. I am moved when I think of the fate of all those who have lost their freedom because of their convictions. I also think of the Jews in the USSR who are not permitted to leave the country."

At these words, Gorbachev raised his hand and for an instant clenched his fist above the golden armrest. He seemed literally to be grasping for the words with which to react to Chirac. Then it was his turn. He stepped forward to reply, his face set. But instead of giving vent to his anger, he let his charm break through. Without wasting time on Chirac's charges, he stuck to his script, praising the beauty of the French capital and the sensitivity of its citizens, and recalling the Paris Communards and Lenin's sojourn in the small flat in the Rue Marie-Rose.

He reacted in an equally restrained manner during the most politically sensitive and the most public part of his visit — the international press conference in the Elysée Palace, the first to be given by a Kremlin leader for a quarter century. President Francois Mitterrand had just rejected Gorbachev's suggestion for separate Franco— Soviet negotiations on the reduction of medium-range nuclear weapons. Gorbachev accepted the slight almost benevolently and with feigned innocence: after all, he said, he was only putting forward a suggestion, a point of discussion, not a demand. Nevertheless, he asserted that the new Soviet disarmament proposals could introduce a new phase in the politics of detente. For, as he had already told the French National Assembly the previous day, security could no longer be guaranteed by military means.

None of his predecessors had ever come close to making such statements, yet Gorbachev was talking not simply to French parliamentarians and the Western public, but also to millions of Soviet television viewers and to his own military commanders. "This is a totally new situation," he said, "which signifies a break with the traditions, the way of thinking and the patterns of behaviour, which have developed over centuries, and even over millennia. The human spirit does not adapt to change immediately, that's true for everyone, including us. We have started to change our way of thinking, and to bring many familiar things utterly and completely into line with reality, including things in the military and, of course, the political fields."

Was Gorbachev announcing a major change of course? Or was this merely a "Gorbat-show" (as *Libération* put it) to lure Europe away from America? No one could say. One thing was clear: he was continuing the long-range duel with the American President which he had started in London in December 1984 and which would be continued at Geneva a few weeks later.

Paris was not a repeat of London. People knew what to expect of him. Against the elitist, protocol-obsessed

French, Gorbachev cut a less statesmanlike figure than he had in Britain. But he never lost his composure, confining himself to short attacks, without falling back on threatening gestures or affected posing. If he sometimes gave abrupt answers to questions about espionage diplomacy, political prisoners, human rights, Jews and exit visas, he was after all speaking not only to the West but also to the millions of viewers in the Soviet Union. Generally, he proved himself persuasive, subtle and flexible.

As an actor, Gorbachev showed that he had matured since London, taking a leaf or two from Reagan's book. He used dramatic pauses with more practice. He lowered his voice more to emphasise the significance of important phrases.

It was also clear that he was much more than a mere actor. In contrast to his predecessors and many a Western head of government, he felt strong enough to admit to weakness. "We are fully conscious of the weaknesses in our work," he told the French parliamentarians, "and of the difficulties and problems which are often quite serious enough." But for that very reason, he said, the Soviet Union needed to keep international relations on an even keel. "We all live in one house," he said, speaking on French television on the eve of his visit, "even though some enter this house through one entrance and others through another entrance. We must co-operate within this house."

Right from the start he sought to win agreement and support from European governments for his attempt to move President Reagan to compromise on SDI. It was to this end that he put forward his proposals to reduce strategic nuclear weapons systems by 50 percent and to negotiate separately with the French and British about their nuclear forces. But then, in answer to accusations that he sought the division of the Atlantic Alliance, he told the French National Assembly, "We are after all realists and we understand completely how strong are the ties — historical, political and economic — that bind Western Europe and the United States." For this reason the delegates should understand that "we are not practising Metternich's politics of the 'balance of power,' setting one state against the others, hammering together bloc and counter-bloc, creating 'axes' and 'triangular alliances,' but rather a policy of global detente." The visit to Paris also made it plain that in establishing good relations with Europe Gorbachev had a secondary aim. Set on long-term reform, he wants to give his own empire a new European identity. First Leningrad, next Paris. If Moscow is to seek technological support from Western Europe, then it is nonsensical for it to seal itself off from the flow of Western information.

The most visible proof of this intention was the unprecedented wealth of uncut, uncensored television transmissions that blanketed the Soviet Union. For the first time ever, Soviet citizens heard on official broadcasts sharp, uncensored questions by Western journalists about political prisoners, human rights and exit visas. In Paris Gorbachev opened further his window to the West.

Finally, Paris was a rehearsal for Geneva. Reagan had announced that he wanted to discuss human rights with Gorbachev. In Paris, the Soviet Party leader prepared both himself and Soviet television viewers for this. He did not shy away from any questions. Seated on a gold-and-green Louis XV chair in a ceremonial hall in the Kremlin, one of France's star TV interviewers asked him: "Is it true that there are four million political prisoners in the Soviet Union?" Gorbachev's answer, transmitted uncut on Soviet television, displayed for the average Russian citizen both righteous indignation and statesmanlike self-control: "Absurd. You know, this reminds one of Goebbels' propaganda. I am very surprised that a modern and educated man like you, Mr. Mourousi, can ask such questions. I repeat: that is absurd!" Gorbachev's response was on target on two counts. Firstly, attack is the best defence; and secondly, although there are several thousand political prisoners in the Soviet Union, a sad enough state of affairs, the number put forward by the interviewer was indeed absurd.

Soviet television viewers even heard about the expulsion for espionage of Soviet diplomats from London in spring

1985. This question caused the Kremlin leader no great embarrassment either. Relaxed and not a little cynical, Gorbachev answered: "Every embassy has instructions to maintain their security. And it is quite normal for an embassy to keep their government informed."

More important were his remarks about emigration, reunification of families, the increased flow of information and the exchange of students within the framework of a pan-European rapprochement. Even if his words were deliberately vague and self-serving, Soviet citizens had never heard anything like them. For the first time, people in the Soviet Union officially heard of the exile in 1980 of Nobel prizewinner Andrei Sakharov and of the 1978 punishment of the human rights campaigner Anatoli Shcharansky. On the penultimate day of his visit, Gorbachev made another novel remark about Sakharov. The case had, he said, been "presented to the appropriate offices for assessment," a further indication that in the run-up to the summit Moscow was sounding out the possibility of giving exit visas to human rights activists.

In conclusion, Gorbachev did not frighten anyone nor did he send the Europeans into confusion, as conservatives of every ilk had prophesied. The Europeans declined to be embraced, but they felt that Gorbachev had no intention of suffocating them.

The actual effects of Gorbachev's visit were limited. London and Bonn came out in support of Star Wars, and a section of the Reagan administration continued to make it plain that a long-term economic upturn on the part of Moscow does not suit their interests.

But Gorbachev's tactics have nevertheless paid dividends. In France, many parliamentarians and publicists distanced themselves further from Washington's Star Wars proposals. It has become clear that the European and the American views about Gorbachev and his strategy for the Soviet Union are diverging. The vast majority of European governments support the attempt to reform the Soviet system, hoping that reform within will involve a limitation of ambitions without.

The Road to Geneva

On November 7 1985, the 68th anniversary of the Revolution, Gorbachev presided over the great annual parade through Red Square. Wearing a light Karakul fur hat and a bright blue scarf, he appeared to promise a more vigorous future. He gave the impression of a man who was equally conscious of his power and his responsibility.

Gorbachev's special position on the stand — at the head of the Military, to the right of the speaker, with the remaining Politburo Members on the speaker's left — demonstrated that he had distanced himself from collective leadership more quickly than any Party leader since Lenin. He was on the verge of his entry onto the world stage. It was 12 days before the Geneva summit.

To observers, the parade seemed to symbolize the Soviet Union's most urgent problem. The soldiers could be seen as an expression of dogged determination to keep pace with the rate of America's rearmament. Yet the parade was in effect a march for a better economy. The banners and signs of the passing columns demanded better quality, higher productivity and better planning. Clearly modernization is in part dependent on reduced arms expenditure, and reductions in military costs are themselves only possible with improved relations with America.

Therein lies the major threat of Reagan's Star Wars dream. For the first time the Soviet Union fears that, although it has so far been able to equal all American innovations in Western technology more quickly than expected, it will be unable to make the leap from simple offensive systems to as yet unknown and cost-intensive defensive systems. All objections to Star Wars can be reduced to one basic formula: Moscow does not wish to have its future overall strategy dictated by the Americans.

Of course, in the past the Soviet Union has always responded to outside pressures with the most extraordinary performances. Should not Star Wars therefore be welcomed as a stimulus to science and technology? In principle, yes. But in practice Soviet resources are too limited and the division between military and civilian research and enterprises too sharp. Computers are needed to automate consumer goods production. If armaments production is geared up with new vigour, then industry will once again lose specialists and new computer hardware to the Military.

Hence Gorbachev's commitment to detente. Even in his first interview (*Pravda* of April 8 1985) the new Party leader told the Americans: "Confrontation is not a congenital defect in our relationships. Rather it is an anomaly, whose existence is by no means inevitable. We not only consider the improvement of Soviet–American relationships to be extremely necessary, but also to be possible." In his first meeting with American parliamentarians, he told the Speaker of the House, Thomas (Tip) O'Neill, "We do not think that the current tensions in our relations are to be equated with a conflict of interests that will inevitably lead to a fatal collision between our countries.... In practice we have seen that mutually advantageous Soviet–American co-operation is perfectly possible." O'Neill was convinced. "They want to negotiate," he said.

Thus Gorbachev quickly gained the initiative in the run-up to Geneva. To achieve his long-term aim, he adopted dramatically different techniques. Always ready to communicate, he combined charm with aggression, pleas with analysis, sweeping schemes with pragmatic proposals.

In a major interview with *Time* magazine, Gorbachev stated confidently: "If all that we are doing is indeed viewed as mere propaganda, why not respond to it according to the principle of 'an eye for an eye and a tooth for a tooth?' We have stopped nuclear explosions. Then you Americans could take revenge by doing likewise. You could deal us yet another propaganda blow, say, by suspending the development of one of your new strategic missiles. And we would respond with the same kind of 'propaganda.' And so on and so forth. Would anyone be harmed by competition in such 'propaganda?' Of course, it could not be a substitute for a comprehensive arms-limitation agreement, but it would be a significant step leading to such an agreement."

The reasoning and the substance of his words were clever and the delivery not without charm. Yet in early November 1985, when Secretary of State George Schultz was making the final preparations for the Geneva summit in Moscow, Gorbachev treated him with unexpected brusqueness. He lectured Schultz. He interrupted the interpreter's translations to contradict Schultz's statements. He showed irritability. All in all, he left the impression that in extended, detailed discussion he preferred to out-talk rather than out-think his opponents.

Although Star Wars was obviously the critical issue to be discussed in Geneva, Gorbachev continued to give signals that he did not want to make the issue the yardstick for the success of the Geneva summit. On November 8, in his answer to a message from the leaders of Sweden, Greece, Tanzania, India, Argentina and Mexico, he announced the Soviet Union's readiness to continue its unilateral moratorium on nuclear weapons tests beyond the original deadline of the end of 1985, if the Americans were prepared to join such a test ban. "There is now a real possibility," he said in the message, "of making a historic step in the fullest sense of the word, so that [nuclear] tests should be halted for all time."

With hindsight, Gorbachev's approach seems a wise one, for the differences between the two men were all too clear. Gorbachev wanted to build up the Soviet Union to become an economic superpower. Reagan wanted to use weapons technology to make America invulnerable. The former could only reach his objective through arms control, the latter only by building new weapons. To expect a reconciliation of such differences was wishful thinking. Success would have to be measured by different terms.

The Fireside Summit

For six long years, the two superpowers had been berating one another as if harking back to the days of the Cold War.

Now their two leaders sat opposite one another, alone except for their interpreters, six times in two days. Their talks were, in Gorbachev's words, "open, full, sharp — at times extremely sharp." Predictably, they hardly solved a single contentious question. But they ended with a remarkable public demonstration of goodwill. How did their meetings go behind the scenes? US and Soviet sources have provided a composite view of events.

The first private meeting — on the morning of Tuesday, November 19 in the Villa Fleur d'Eau, on the shores of Lake Geneva — was planned to take 15 minutes. But the two men spoke for an hour and four minutes. They thus instantly stepped from the path laid down by protocol. Each delivered a 20-minute monologue about relations between the two superpowers. Reagan bemoaned the lack of mutual trust which inhibited both from making the "leap of faith" to peace. Gorbachev agreed, but he accused the Americans of feeding this mistrust with "myths" about the Soviet Union. He said the military–industrial complex, which was closely linked with the American government, spread the fantasy that the Soviet Union was a threat in order to secure the highest possible defence expenditure. The think-tanks of the Heritage Foundation in Washington and the Hoover Institute in California wanted to see the Soviet economy in ruins. For Reagan, this pinpointed one of those misunderstandings that had to be clarified. The armaments industry was a significant, but not the decisive factor in the American economy, he said. He himself considered it a mistake to want to damage the Soviet economy. Governments that tried to manipulate economies would only damage themselves.

The theme of national mistrust quickly led the two men to their regional rivalries. Reagan described the number of Soviet advisers in Nicaragua as "unacceptable." Nor had Soviet advisers any right to be in Afghanistan, Ethiopia and Angola. "No right!" he insisted. "This is Soviet aggression. It is a destabilizing act."

Gorbachev replied, "There is no basis for this assertion. Absolutely none. These are people who are conducting a

national war of liberation." The Soviet constitution prescribed that people must be helped to attain freedom. "The
Americans," he argued (both then, and later at his press
conference at the conclusion of the summit), "view the
Soviet Union as the sole cause of all the problems in the
Third World. We say to them: things are not that simple.
The Soviet Union is not behind every crisis. But this is
what they believe and they base their policies on this
assumption. Only: how do they explain Vietnam?"

On this point, he spoke forcefully. But on Afghanistan he
picked his words carefully. He avoided mentioning American support for resistance groups. And he let Reagan
know that he had not blundered into this problem on his
own, and that he was working for a diplomatic solution.
Soviet troops were not intended to stay in Afghanistan
indefinitely.

On the afternoon of the first day they had their longest
and most forceful discussion on the subject which divides
them most: Star Wars, Ronald Reagan's Strategic Defence
Initiative. The American President opened this debate
with a half-hour lecture on the "uncivilized nature" of a
doctrine which maintains peace by the threat of mutual
destruction. "I am aware of your fear that SDI is only a
pretext to achieve a first-strike capability," said Reagan.
"That is a legitimate concern. For that reason I want to
explain my 'open-labs' idea to you." Gorbachev tried to
interrupt several times, but Reagan insisted on carrying
his thoughts through to the end. They led to the already
well-known assurance that he firmly intended to make SDI
technology available to Moscow once it was developed.

When Reagan had finished, Gorbachev held him with a
thoughtful look, answering only after a long silence: "I
have understood completely what you have said. It does not
convince me. It is emotional. It is a dream. Who can control
it? Who can keep a grip on it? It opens up space for the
arms race." A space system that could overcome nuclear
weapons was, in short, incredible. It still seemed more
likely that Reagan planned to use his defence system as a
shield, to allow an American first strike. "You may dream

of peace," Gorbachev said, "but we have to look at reality. I am not a blood-thirsty person. We must reduce all weapons and not create new ones."

Reagan interjected: "But if we combine this with our 'open-labs,' then our scientists can see what you are doing. And you can see what we are doing."

But Gorbachev was unmoved: "We must ban the introduction of all space weapons," he insisted. "Ban them! Ban all space weapons!"

Tempers began to rise. "When we had a monopoly on nuclear weapons," Reagan said, "we did not use it, as I have already told you. Why don't you trust me?"

"Would you trust me, if I said that the Soviet Union would never attack the United States?" Gorbachev replied. "As a leader, I can't take it on faith alone! We won't be run out of the game! We should negotiate now! A year or 18 months from now, it will be more difficult!"

After finishing his plea, Gorbachev leant back and spoke more calmly. "You can see that I am getting very agitated about all this," he said, and then after a pause added: "It looks as though we have arrived at a dead end."

At this moment, just when the relationship might have broken down, Reagan suggested some fresh air, a walk down to a small hut on the edge of the lake. Clearly, the suggestion was not entirely spontaneous, for when the two men arrived, the fire was already alight. It was this intimate touch that gave the meeting its name: the Fireside Summit.

Sitting by the fire, looking out at the lake, the two continued to discuss the militarization of space, but in more muted tones and in generalities. The President also used the opportunity to present Gorbachev with a paper in Russian containing Washington's proposals for a reduction of strategic weapons by 50 percent. Gorbachev studied the document with concentration, and then answered laconically that this would not ban SDI (privately, the Kremlin leader spoke of SDI, and not of Star Wars, as he did in public). Reagan confirmed that SDI would and must continue. In that case, stated Gorbachev flatly, there would be no agreement.

Again, that might have been the end. This time it was Gorbachev who bridged the gap. "We must continue talking about it," he said. Reagan agreed. On the return from the small hut to the villa, he said: "I want to invite you to come and visit me in the United States next year." "And I want to invite you to come to the Soviet Union," answered Gorbachev. "I accept," said Reagan; "I accept," Gorbachev echoed. They shook hands with a smile, and the mood lifted.

The next day, the two men discussed human rights. Gorbachev reacted calmly. He explained in detail what the Soviet leadership understood by human rights: a roof over everyone's head, work for all, free health care — these were rights, according to Gorbachev, which not everyone had in America. Reagan countered this by saying that he wanted to see action, not hear propaganda. Despite these firm assertions, each obviously gained a certain understanding of the other's point of view.

Before the two leaders read their final communiques in the International Conference Centre on the snowy morning of November 21, Reagan whispered to Gorbachev: "I bet the hawks in both our countries will have bleeding hearts if we shake hands here." Strange words for a President who had risen to popularity with harsh warnings about showing any trust towards communists. Caught between the principle of not giving an inch on his anti-communism and his promise to go half-way to ensure peace, Reagan appeared to want to demonstrate that he could balance both demands. In the President's words, he could not claim to agree with Gorbachev on ideology and national objectives "but we do understand one another better now, and that is the key to peace... he is looking for solutions just as honestly as we are." Gorbachev too was on the horns of a dilemma: he could not prevent Star Wars, yet he had to continue to try to do so. He needed to appear to believe in the ultimate success of patient negotiation in order not to seem to be leaving Geneva empty-handed.

The two superpowers did not come an inch closer on the

decisive question of arms control. The American President did not even acknowledge the Soviet test moratorium to be a good start. The ABM treaty of 1972, which has become the foundation of Soviet arguments against the arms race in space, was not even mentioned in the common communique. Initially, nothing points to a growing readiness on Reagan's part to rein in America's defence industries. The SDI programme appears indispensable for their continued expansion, because the market for conventional nuclear warheads and missiles is generally satisfied.

Yet the feeling of the summit remained positive. In large measure, this was Gorbachev's doing. He had no real expectation that he could prevent SDI then and there. He therefore tidily separated those issues that lay in an uncertain future, beyond his political influence, from those he could affect.

In doing so he had two main objectives.

In the short term, he wished to model himself as a new kind of Soviet leader in time for the 27th Party Congress in February 1986 — confident, responsible and realistic in his dealings with America. For decades, the Soviets have had a fixation about equality with the Americans. It flattered the Kremlin immensely when President Nixon acknowledged Soviet parity as a world power in 1972, and was correspondingly hurtful when Carter and Reagan withdrew this "honour." Now the wound was healed. The common communique implied a recognition of equality, a recognition that served to counter the fact that the summit failed to stop SDI. Gorbachev could thus present himself to the Party Congress, after less than a year in office, as an equal to the American President, a man who knew the value of national strength. For the vast majority of Soviet citizens, such a display of self-confidence by their Party leader — especially after the decrepitude of his predecessors — is far more important than the details of arms control.

His domestic aims were aided by the emergence of Raisa as a public figure. In a Soviet context, it is a breakthrough for the media to present the General Secretary's wife as an independent personality. Her appearances — laying the

corner-stone of the Museum of the Red Cross, for instance
— were given special reports. These were evidence both of
Gorbachev's interest in her political role — her performance seemed to signal an increasing participation in social
decision-making by Soviet women — and of her potential
influence on the Party leader. Almost certainly, Gorbachev
wishes to revive that long-buried Leninist tradition by
which women played a role in public life, recalling the
status once enjoyed by Nadezhda Krupskaya, Inessa
Armand, Alexandra Kollontai, Elena Stassova, Yevgenia
Bosch and many others.

In the long term, Gorbachev's objective was to use this
summit as a foundation to prepare a lasting relationship
with the United States, one that would endure long after
Reagan. He wants to train up the younger Soviet elite in a
new way of dealing with America, avoiding crises and
promoting contacts to help modernize their own system.
What is more, the new relationship is intended to be somewhat independent of a breakthrough in arms control. Gorbachev himself had recognized considerably earlier that
there could be no guarantee of security by gambling on
arms control, only by building a stronger economy.

Moscow's insistence that there could be no improvement
in Soviet–US relations without the prior removal of SDI
was Gromyko's legacy. With the Geneva summit, Gorbachev set that legacy aside. Admittedly the Soviet Party
leader said, "We are prepared for a radical reduction of
nuclear weapons on condition that the door is firmly shut
to the development of an arms race in space." And he let
there be no doubt that Moscow would counter an unhindered continuation of the SDI programme by building more
offensive weapons. But he added that this "is not our political choice. [We would like] the USA to rethink the whole
situation, despite everything." By implying that the Americans have not gone far enough in their thinking, he has
left himself an opportunity to appeal further to the American Congress, the media and the Western allies. As
Yevgeni Velikhov, Vice President of the Academy of Sciences, put it: "Reagan does not make the ultimate decision.

That is in the hands of Congress and public opinion."

Though unable to stop the arms race in its tracks, Gorbachev has at least loosened the hide-bound relationship between Washington and Moscow. Realizing that Reagan's SDI programme can only be reduced, not prevented, he no longer relies only on attempts to drum up support against Star Wars in other countries. He no longer wants to by-pass America, but to convince it of its global responsibility (as he sees it).

This is a policy that paid immediate dividends in Eastern Europe. In proclaiming the concept of a community of responsibility, he recalled the very model for limiting arms expenditure that some nations of Eastern and Western Europe created while the two superpowers were still incapable of dialogue. This explains the enthusiastic response Gorbachev received when, immediately after the summit, he briefed his allies in Prague.

At home, too, he gained in authority. He needed all the authority he could muster to justify signing a declaration by which Soviet interests are not fully protected. As he himself candidly told the 1,500 delegates of the Supreme Soviet: "The solution of the most important matters — those involving the cessation of the arms race — were not achieved at the meeting. The stockpiles of weapons will not be reduced as a result of the summit. The arms race will continue."

In these circumstances, control of the Military becomes a vital matter. On this issue hinges the success of Gorbachev's plans for both economic reform and improved international relations.   •

The General Secretary and the Generals

Without doubt, the Military were not among Gorbachev's supporters at his accession. At Chernenko's funeral, Gorbachev gave the address — his first public speech as General Secretary — without a military representative by his side.

There are good historical reasons for this stand-off. It is

traditional for Russian elites to try to maintain as large an
army as possible and to give them as little say as possible.
The tsarist empire was held together by the Military, but
was never ruled by officers. The new Kremlin leaders' fear
of excessively strong generals is as old as the Soviet empire
itself. One major problem has always been how political
control of the Army is to be reconciled with the unimpeded
development of its military efficacy. The dilemma has continually led to intervention in the power structure. In 1937
Stalin had his Minister of War Tukhachevsky shot because
the highly-regarded marshal was supposedly preparing a
coup d'etat. A third of the officer corps, 13 out of 15 Army
generals, and three out of five marshals fell victims to
Stalin's secret police. The officers had their revenge later,
when they helped to put Stalin's Security Service chief,
Lavrenti Beria, to death. In his memoirs, Khrushchev complained: "Who in our country is in a position to fill the
leadership with fear? It is the Military." Relations between
the Security Service and the Army today are incomparably
better than they were, but they are still precarious.

The one man who allayed the Kremlin's fears, who knew
how to unify political control and military efficacy, was
Dmitri Fyodorovich Ustinov. The Defence Minister, who
held his office for eight years, died in December 1984, aged
76. As a loyal soldier of the Party, though never a professional soldier, Ustinov, with his ash blond hair, crumpled
face and thick glasses, was the ideal custodian of military
power. Yet he kept a sense of proportion, authorizing no
more arms than the Party wanted and the economy could
bear, despite the demands of the Military. Under his predecessor, Defence Minister Andrei Grechko, he was the administrator of the armaments programme that allowed Moscow almost to close the weapons gap with Washington.

In the Politburo itself, there was no competent successor
for Ustinov — an indication of how little the Party elite
and the military leadership were linked. The decision to
groom Marshal Sergei Sokolov, a conservative but colourless veteran, to be Ustinov's successor confirmed the ing-
enuity with which the Kremlin inner leadership sought to

ensure that the Party would continue to control the Military. Sokolov was no more than a member of the Central Committee, until he became a Candidate Member of the Politburo in April. But he was too distant from the centre of power and too old to play an influential role.

On July 10, four months after his election as General Secretary, Gorbachev announced his programme to the Army leadership in Minsk. This speech was neither televised nor published. Undoubtedly, though, he emphasised the primacy of the Party, a policy then put into effect with a series of dramatic changes of personnel.

The following weekend, there were abrupt changes in East Germany, which were given wide coverage there and none at all in the Soviet Union. The Supreme Commander of the Group of Soviet Forces in Germany, Army General Mikhail Zaitsev, and his senior political officer, General Alexei Lizichev, were ordered back to Moscow. Lizichev, a general of Gorbachev's generation, then replaced the Red Army's senior political watch-dog, 77-year-old General Alexei Yepishev, appointed in 1962.

The line which the current Kremlin leadership expects of its new generation of generals has been spelled out by a General Staff colonel, M.A. Gareyev, in a remarkable book on the great Civil War commander Mikhail Frunze. The book, *Frunze as Military Theoretician*, appeared at the time of Gorbachev's accession to power. Gareyev emphasises that "military theory must continually strive to limit resources for military purposes strictly to what is wholly necessary, so that defence becomes reliable and, at the same time, not too burdensome for the state." This book was additionally notable because it was praised in review by an officer of far higher rank than the author: Army General Pyotr Lushev, the long-serving Commander-in-Chief of the Moscow Military District, the very man who in July 1985 succeeded Zaitsev as commander-in-chief in East Germany.

By the end of the year, Gorbachev had also replaced the commanders-in-chief of the two military areas responsible for strategic offensive weapons: the Rocket Troops and the

Fleet (which also contains the 62 nuclear submarines).

First the 71-year-old commander of the Rocket Troops, Marshal of the Artillery Vladimir Tolubko, was replaced by Yuri Maximov, ten years his junior, who previously had had nothing to do with missile units, but who had already been promoted to Army general under Andropov.

Then on December 11 1985 the Army newspaper *Red Star* briefly reported that the Commander-in-Chief of the Soviet Navy, named as the Deputy Defence Minister Admiral V.N. Chernavin, had flown off to visit Tunisia. The report meant that the previous commander, 75-year-old Admiral Sergei Georgievich Gorshkov, the creator and strategist of modern Soviet sea power, had been dismissed without a word of appreciation. Over the previous 30 years, Gorshkov had built up and commanded the greatest battle fleet in the world. In increasing the Soviet fleet, however, he had also revealed its defects. It has no reliable bases outside of the Soviet Union. Despite its size, it would, in case of conflict, be easy to cut off, its vessels becoming sitting ducks to modern weapons like Cruise missiles. In addition, the American Star Wars programme would force vessels to become sea-based — but the vessels would be submarines, not the heavy battleships in which Gorshkov had invested.

Understandably then, Gorbachev's new Commander-in-Chief of the Navy is a man from the submarine fleet. Born in 1928, in 1962 Vladimir Nikolaievich Chernavin became the captain of one of the first Soviet nuclear submarines from which a missile was launched under water. As a staff officer in 1966, Chernavin took part in the first circumnavigation of the globe by Soviet submarines, for which he was given the Order of Lenin. In 1981, *Red Star* emphasised his qualities; "Today's naval commander must have the qualities of an experienced politician, the willpower of a hardened fighter, the breadth of knowledge of a scientist and the patience of a teacher. At all times he must be a Bolshevik and a Leninist.... Such a man is Admiral Chernavin."

With the appointment of Chernavin and Maximov, Gorbachev could simultaneously strengthen his position in the National Defence Council. His views are also represented there by Prime Minister Ryzhkov, chief ideologist Ligachev, KGB Director Chebrikov and Foreign Minister Shevardnadze. Chief of the General Staff Akhromeyev is likely to steer a middle course. State President Gromyko and Defence Minister Sokolov (about both of whom rumours of resignation were already circulating at the end of 1985), as well as Marshals Kulikov and Petrov, form the opposition, favouring a reduction in detente and increased armaments expenditure. All in all, the Party, the KGB and the new generation of leaders had clearly gained the upper hand over the old military guard.

Will peace and common sense have a better chance under Gorbachev against automatic rearmament and the superpowers' irrational rivalry? Is Gorbachev good not only for Russia, but also for the rest of the world? The answer is a conditional yes — especially if the West helps him.

He is ambitious for power — not power for its own sake, but power to improve his own society. He cannot do this by constantly fending off foreign challenges, real or imagined. He needs Western support in the removal of such threats. In a very real sense, therefore, the West now has an opportunity to contribute to a better life for the average Soviet citizen. Perhaps — just perhaps — in years to come rivalry between the superpowers will be expressed in economic rather than military terms, to the benefit of both.

APPENDIX 1

The Prospects for Economic Reform

by Mária Huber

Under Brezhnev, the impulse for change had flagged. State and Party leadership no longer aimed at reforms but only at improvements in the economic mechanism. Andropov launched a spectacular campaign to improve labour discipline, with a view to increasing productivity. If the economic growth of the Soviet Union increasingly depends on higher productivity (intensive growth), this suggests that sources of growth other than those relating to productivity (extensive growth) are gradually being exhausted.

Published figures support this view. According to an estimate by A.G. Aganbegyan, for many years Director of the Academy's Institute for Economics and Organization of Industrial Production in Novosibirsk and now Gorbachev's special economics adviser, resources — manpower, natural wealth and investments — can ensure a growth rate of 2 percent at best. The annual growth rates of the national revenue between 1981 and 1985 amounted to 3 percent, the 1 percent difference being due to improved efficiency. But now the rate of increase in productivity is declining.

Because of the poor prospects for growth, Gorbachev is now calling for "profound restructuring of the economy and of the entire system." In nearly every speech he urges "intensive development," which includes: accelerated scientific and technological progress, reorganization of investment policy and economic management, economical use of resources, improvement in the quality and organization of work, and strict discipline at the workplace. In agriculture, he urges the use of chemicals, mechanization, and the planting of new crops.

These requirements — set out in the *Principal Directions of the Economic and Social Development of the USSR for the Years 1986 to 1990 and for the Period up to 2000* — are nothing new in principle. For 20 years the Soviet Union has seen itself as being in "transition from extensive to intensive economic growth." Gorbachev's predecessors, however, failed to create the conditions for this. That is why most Western experts continue to be sceptical; in their view the only way in which the new Party chief can hope to achieve his main objective — the modernization of the Soviet Union — is by resorting to supply-and-demand mechanisms.

Can the new Party boss achieve what his predecessors have failed to achieve — to create the structural conditions for increased productivity? Where should he start, and what should he aim for?

His statements suggest that he aims to build on the economic reform of 1965, a reform which may have petered out but which has not remained without some consequences. The relevant Central Committee Resolution of September 1965 aimed to accelerate technological progress and raise material prosperity. To that end new ways of measuring production were introduced in central and enterprise-level planning. These changes in planning criteria and methods did not, however, enhance the independence of enterprises to any marked extent. But they did create a basis for "rational" economic decisions. Until then, production targets had focused on "catching up with and overtaking the capitalist economy," regardless of economic or social cost. Now, enterprises and authorities were to take into account that planning included accountancy. To cut costs and to increase productivity, however, were totally unfamiliar tasks to management. In point of fact, many of these tasks were insoluble because the price structure was too rigid and had long been overtaken by demand for investment and consumer goods. Responsibility for adjusting capacity to changing needs was in the hands of the ministries, which from the outset obstructed the decentralization of decision-making.

Nevertheless, the independence of enterprises did increase quite substantially. The 1965 reform enabled them to apply up to 20 percent of the (now rapidly rising) enterprise profits to the payment of bonuses and social benefits to their work-force as well as to infrastructure and modernization. Again the ministries at once came up with directives and regulations. But they were unable to prevent the workers' wages, *enhanced by the new bonuses*, and hence also their purchasing power, from greatly exceeding the *planned* level of wages and, in consequence, the supply of goods made available (see Tables 1 and 2, summarizing data from *Narodnoye Khozyaystvo SSR 1982*, Moscow, 1983. Currently, 1 rouble = c. £1 or $1.4).

Table 1: *Industrial Funds Available for Incentives (million roubles).*

	1970	1975	1980	1982
Bonus fund	3,739	5,663	6,714	7,202
Social and cultural fund	1,620	1,764	2,251	2,471
Modernization fund	3,341	5,405	7,251	7,279
TOTAL	8,700	12,832	16,216	16,952

Table 2: *Average Monthly Wage (roubles).*

	1970	1975	1980	1982
Manual and office workers:				
Economy as a whole	122	146	169	177
Industry	133	162	185	196
Agriculture	101	127	149	159
In industry:				
Manual workers	131	161	186	197
Technical intelligentsia	178	199	213	220
Office workers	112	131	146	152

The data show that industrial enterprises almost doubled the overall amounts in their incentive funds between 1970 and 1982. Over that period the real earnings of manual and office workers rose by 40 percent.

In fact, the relationship between incentives and results is not direct. Since the mid-1970's, the development of the incentive funds began to clash with the Party's unchanged priorities.

There is more point in analysing these conflicts than in continually reciting the familiar examples of supply bottlenecks and black labour in the Soviet Union. Comparisons with the West are easy to make — their low standard of living, our high one; their inefficient planned economy, our rationality and competition; on their side the rule of a Party and planning bureaucracy, on ours free enterprise. High levels of consumption and a high level of adaptive dynamism in a dozen Western countries are often elevated into yardsticks of a well-functioning economy. But the queues outside Moscow shops have their counterparts in the rows of people on the benches of German, British and American labour exchanges and social welfare offices. It seems that the satisfaction of basic needs in a high-efficiency competition oriented economy is no more universally possible than it is in a bureaucratic and in many respects backward system. Judgements based on such obvious differences lead to over-simplifications, and to an underestimation of potential for development.

It is more instructive to concentrate on those Soviet economic shortcomings that are amenable to correction. (It is of course necessary to bear in mind the differences between the systems. The socialist economic system, for example, rejects the high unemployment accepted in Western countries as the consequence of "progress." That refusal acts as a brake on the mobility of labour. Fear of dismissal does not enhance discipline or performance in the Soviet economy.)

The measures initiated after 1965 for the improvement of planning methods and for a widening of autonomy have been assessed by most Western experts on the Soviet economy as "half-hearted reforms." Donna Gold and John P. Hardt of the Research Department of the US Congress, on the other hand, believe that if one accepts a step-by-step approach to change or to performance improvement then even some modest steps may produce results. Substantial improvements need not depend on a total transformation of the economy.

In order to discover Gorbachev's possible points of departure in his endeavours to achieve "substantial improvements" we have to consider the three areas in which the Soviet leadership can hope to be effective: economic policy; economic mechanism; and economic system.

1. ECONOMIC POLICY

In the area of economic policy, measures of control include changes in foreign trade, in labour legislation and, of particular significance, in investment targets.

Foreign Trade

During the 1970's, the Soviet Union's foreign trade with the West increased threefold. Among the capitalist industrialized countries, West Germany holds first place (by a wide margin) as a trade partner. German trade with the Soviet Union increased by 8.6 percent in 1984 to reach a value of 25.1 billion D-Marks (approximately 6.8 billion pounds sterling). A point has now been reached when a further increase in the exchange of consumer and industrial goods urgently requires direct contacts between firms. At the beginning of 1985, Oleg T. Bogomolov, the Director of the Institute for the Economics of the Socialist World System, in a lecture in Vienna announced that the Soviet Union would make it possible for joint-venture companies to be set up with capitalist enterprises. If, in the foreseeable future, managers of Soviet enterprises are really to be permitted to negotiate with Western firms direct — as the Novosibirsk economists have been demanding for some time — an important step towards decentralization will have been taken.

The *Principal Directions of Economic and Social Development*, as published on November 9 1985, envisages only "direct production links with enterprises in the fraternal countries as well as the creation of joint enterprises." But trade relations with the industrialized capitalist countries are to be likewise intensified. The joint resolution of the Central Committee and of the Council of Ministers of July 1985 — which followed a spectacular conference of top-level Party and economic officials, managers and economic experts — for the first time foresaw the promotion of exports at enterprise level. Prices of exported goods could be adjusted by up to 20 percent, and enterprises may use a portion of their dollar income from exports to buy modern technology and plant from abroad. The VAZ automobile works in the town of Togliatti is already making use of this facility.

Labour Legislation

The Soviet Constitution and labour legislation have recently given considerably more automony to work-forces and their planning and production organizations. That is a considerable step forward, even though it is still a far cry from equal rights between work-force and management. From oppression to partnership is a long road.

According to the social planning concept — as elaborated by research institutes with a view to enhancing job satisfaction and motivation — enterprise work-forces will not only be the objects of planning but will also participate in the plans. The people in the enterprises, formerly regarded as "tiny screws in the economic mechanism" — these are the words of the so-called Novosibirsk Research Paper, drafted at the Siberian Branch of the USSR Academy of Sciences for a "closed seminar" of economic experts held in Moscow in April 1983 — were now to assume a new role in the shaping of their working conditions. The formal prerequisites for this were provided by law in June 1983. This did not, however, receive much attention in practice, as Gorbachev complained in a speech to Party ideology officials 18 months later, in December 1984. His criticism — the subject of a *Pravda* editorial immediately after his election as General Secretary (*Pravda*, March 17 1985) — reflects the importance he attaches to group interests.

In the face of the well-established mechanisms of economic planning and management, however, he will find it difficult to set new objectives. Old structures and entrenched attitudes favour passivity in the work-place, the levelling of wages and the avoidance of conflict.

Those 8–10 percent of Soviet workers who, according to my estimate, have exercised their rights (Soviet sources speak of 40–60 percent), are merely beginning to acquire that level of information and readiness for conflict without which any shared decision-making envisaged by the law must remain on paper.

Investment targets

In all economic systems, investments are regarded as decisive for the establishment of an effective economic structure. Gorbachev's economic programme gives priority to mechanical engineering, consumer goods and agriculture, even though heavy industry continues officially to enjoy priority. His drive towards a rethinking on economic problems is a vital prerequisite of both improved living standards and technological modernization. In pursuing these two objectives, he is taking up the threads of the economic reform of 1965 — a reform that foundered on the shoals of a number of related inadequacies and abuses.

The reform policy of 1965 was forced on the Soviet leadership because economic growth had dramatically slowed. This proved that the class struggle was not nearly as much of a driving force in the development of a socialist mode of production as Stalin had taught. After the collectivization of agriculture and the levelling of wages in industry, the system could hardly become any more socialist. The "scientific-technological revolution" and the "steadily growing needs of the population" were therefore acknowledged as the driving forces of progress.

In spite of that ideological turn-about two decades ago, Party and state have so far preferred to improve the distribution of scarce commodities rather than to adapt their production to demand, either quantitatively or qualitatively. The purely administrative allocation of raw materials and primary products — occasionally also of consumer goods — has continued to be deeply rooted in a planning system whose foundations were laid in times of extreme shortages and maximum ambitions. Instead of being based on monetary calculations and clearly stated needs, the system was, and is, based on barter and personal contacts. Out of self-interest, the distribution bureaucracy stifles all attempts to overcome the shortages. The lack of contractual relations between enterprises provide plausible arguments for further strengthening the authority of state commissions and ministries.

Even so, as average wage increases show, control has for some time been slipping away from the ministries. The 1965 reform brought enormous, and sometimes rapid, improvements in incomes for individual groups of workers and for a somewhat arbitrary string of enterprises.

Wherever the regulations or the ministries permitted only the "planned" (i.e. slight) improvements in income, production requirements were lowered, by tacit agreement between enterprise managements and individual groups of workers. Performance was thus adjusted downwards with respect to wages. Both these trends resulted in an increasing imbalance between supply and demand. Wages increased, but there was (relatively) less to buy. The consequence was that, from the mid-1970's onwards, corruption flourished as never before.

Any successful struggle against corruption, of the kind started by Andropov and continued now by Gorbachev, therefore demands a considerable extension of the supply of goods. Tatyana Zaslavskaya, a leading member of the staff of the Novosibirsk Academy's Institute, in 1981 put forward the thesis that a system of material incentives can be effective only if goods and services are available to meet the increased purchasing power.

More consumer goods and better services are also vital in the struggle against alcoholism. This is what the new Chairman of the State Planning Commission (Gosplan) Nikolai Talyzin, told the deputies of the Supreme Soviet in November 1985. Talyzin had taken this post over shortly before from Nikolai Baybakov and has since been appointed First Deputy Chairman of the Council of Ministers as well as a Candidate Member of the Politburo. He is one of those new men in the supreme leadership who are expected, in Gorbachev's words, to accomplish "profound analyses, courageous decisions and energetic action" to ensure social and economic reforms.

His task is a hard one. Previously, industry was "not prepared for the changed demand from the public or for a growing call for high-quality goods," Baybakov had told the same forum a year earlier. In spite of repeated announcements since the late 1970's that consumption would be raised, no conceptual changes in economic planning or control came out of Gosplan. Over the past five years the supply of consumer goods had grown at an average of below 4 percent.

In many republics the retail trade targets were not reached, Talyzin admitted. His listeners and readers were bound to know from the press the special efforts made by retail trade to implement its turnover plan in the face of dwindling supplies and a shortage of fresh foodstuffs. During the past few years it had become the practice to put alcoholic drinks on the shelves intended for vegetables and meat. By this means, the shops encouraged alcoholism while fulfilling their turnover plans. Inhabitants of small and remote settlements, for instance, wrote to *Pravda* that instead of urgently needed articles of daily use and foodstuffs they would receive hundreds of cases of vodka and cognac. There was no way of sending those deliveries back. Enormous stocks of alcoholic beverages built up. Drunkenness flourished, work suffered, production fell behind the plan.

The effects of alcoholism on the economy are alarming. The comprehensive measures introduced by Gorbachev in his fight against public enemy No. 1 included administrative restrictions on the sale and production of alcohol and an economic counter-incentive: alcohol sales are no longer included in calculating bonuses due upon the fulfilment of plans.

The programme for "a further enhancement of the people's wellbeing" is designed, simultaneously, to shield the public from damage and to promote the restructuring of the economy. It was formulated in a programme unique in Soviet economic and social history, the "Complex Programme for the Development of the Production of Consumer Goods and the Services Sector for the Years 1986 to 2000." Accordingly, production of consumer goods is to increase by as much as 30 percent during the first five-year period (1986–90), "mainly through intensification of production on the basis of improved organization and full use of existing capacity."

The programme aims at "perfecting the production and consumption of light industry goods, cultural and domestic articles, reacting in good time to changes in public demand, and taking better account of socio-economic changes in enterprises, daily life and in the leisure of the urban and rural population. The primary task of those industries which manufacture such articles is a fundamental improvement in the quality and range of products, the enhancement of their technological and design standard and their efficient performance."

This was followed by a huge list of categories of goods, institutions and services, with numerical data on production, sales and capacity to be reached by the end of the planning period. Production of footwear, for example, is to be increased to 900 million pairs per annum; demand for building materials and sanitary equipment is to be met in full by 1990; the scale of services for recuperation and spa treatment for working people is to be increased by 25–30 percent by 1990; and "measures are to be taken to create the conditions for an extensive supply of legal advice services at industrial and construction enterprises as well as on collective and state farms."

The programme does not provide for the development of market-economy control mechanisms. Expansion of consumption does not imply any assimilation to a Western type of consumer society. The socialist planned economy does not reckon to create abundance. A universal, regular supply of consumer goods means only that production exceeds average demand.

The "Complex Programme" — seen as complementing the foodstuffs programme adopted in 1982 — takes its cue from "scientifically supported norms of consumption." It also calls for knowledge of — indeed, the encouragement of — demand in order to harmonize supply and demand more effectively. Tacitly, the consumer goods plan concedes a greater role to "steadily growing demand" than manufacturing enterprises had envisaged in the past. These find it hard to grasp that a wide choice of consumer goods should occupy the same rank as heavy machinery or the "semi-finished goods necessary to the national economy as a whole."

On October 3 1985, *Izvestiya* admitted that in the current production system — vertically structured according to narrowly defined branches of industry — one out of two or three enterprises (with the exception of a few light industries) produces nothing "for the market." The paper said the economy's inability to meet requirements for shoes and clothes while space projects were being successfully implemented had a heavy material and moral cost to society.

The long-term plan described in *Principal Directions* now pre-scribes that the contribution made by heavy and defence indus-tries to supplying the public with high-quality industrial goods as well as modern electrical household appliances must be "substan-tially increased." Particular importance is attached by the plan to a better supply of goods and services as well as infrastructure for the rural population, and on increasing cultural and leisure faci-lities. To this end a "rational and, for the public, more favourable location of the trade network" should be established.

However, the effect of such measures on improving supplies and efficiency would remain limited without the development of a productive infrastructure. Industry and agriculture are suffering from lack of transport, storage and distribution capacity; and this greatly reduces the efficiency of the economic process.

Pre-war and post-war industrial policy caused gigantic all-round enterprises to spring up, enterprises which were virtually independent of suppliers. But the more numerous these enter-prises became, the more painfully felt was the backwardness in the development of service enterprises and communications net-works. Underdeveloped infrastructure is one of the main reasons for the inflexibility and immobility of the Soviet economy, for the low degree of specialization, and for heavy losses.

The Novosibirsk economic journal *EKO* in its issue No. 2/1981 demonstrated that in 1975 the USA had approximately six times the amount of rail tracks, highways and oil pipelines as the USSR. The Soviet transport network for merchandise and oil was, according to these calculations, a quarter the size the Amer-ican network had been 25 years ago.

In addition to the inadequate development of the transport network, major upheavals in transport are also caused by the antiquated state of transport installations. In spite of rising costs, performance remains low. There is not even a unified concept of road haulage. About 80 percent of all freight is carried by trucks — largely fulfilling the needs only of the enterprises and depart-ments owning the trucks. In Moscow alone, according to *Pravda* of May 26 1985, there are over 1,500 transport enterprises. Many of these are under-used, while others are over-burdened. Although the streets of the city are overcrowded with trucks, haulage requirements are not met. Reorganization — i.e. concen-tration and specialization of truck fleets — would free some 8,000 trucks and drivers.

Principal Directions therefore focuses on the need to use avail-able resources fully, to co-ordinate all means of transport, and to accelerate technical modernization. Investments in rail and road transport are to be increased. Production infrastructure is to be "developed at an accelerated pace."

In the forthcoming Five-Year Plan, however, the "accelerated development" of mechanical engineering holds a clear priority. This industry will, according to the plan, lay the foundations of a modern technology, increased productivity and higher quality. Under Gorbachev, economic policy has clearly acquired the features of selective development, and this should help to overcome antiquated economic structures. In an example of new thinking, the preferential development of mechanical engineering will serve the special needs of small production units, especially of auxiliary agricultural enterprises, of trade, of the hotel and restaurant industry, and of the services sector. Modernization therefore will not be confined to increasing the efficiency of large-scale industry.

Principal Directions stressed the social aims of technological development, in particular the improvement of working conditions. Since the end of the 1970's, the Central Committee has often resolved to reduce the amount of manual, unskilled, unhealthy and heavy physical work, but the resolutions have largely remained on paper.

At enterprise level, such tasks as improving the capacity and facilities for recreation were gradually included in the "plans for the social development of the work-force" from the late 1960's. But their realization has failed, except in a small number of enterprises. It was realized that no substantial improvement in living and working conditions was possible unless the capacity and organization of relevant regional authorities were greatly enlarged. Now *Principal Directions* as well as the "Complex Programme" have placed responsibility for supplies of goods and services in the hands of the Party and administrative bodies of the Union republics.

It is evidently hoped that the development of the social infrastructure, of the health service and of welfare for the aged and disabled will arrest the increasing deterioration of cultural facilities and health care. Soviet sociologists and Party officials have been recording increasing social tensions and a decline in social activity by the public as a direct consequence of the uneven distribution of resources between economic and social goals. At one of its first meetings under Gorbachev's leadership, the Politburo, invoking proposals from working people, directed "that measures should be worked out for improving medical care and social insurance and for developing horticulture."

On the issue of regional and social development, the Gosplan planning directives worked out under Baybakov invariably revealed total ignorance. They preserved the old principle of planning by sector and quantity. Even when Party directives called for new concepts and new indicators, principles applying to extensive growth remained in force. Small wonder that in the summer of 1985 Gorbachev rejected the first draft of the new Five-Year Plan — an unprecedented action and one which seriously discredited Baybakov and Premier Tikhonov.

2. ECONOMIC MECHANISM

To adjust the economic mechanism to the requirements of intensive growth was Kosygin's aim in 1965. It concentrated on the enterprises themselves, in line with the principal task — to decentralize by rationalizing planning and production.

The results of the 1965 reform have been much analysed, and remain controversial. It emerged that the principal problem had been not so much the lack of independence of individual enterprises — as Western economists usually emphasise — as the inability to co-ordinate local economic activities. Regional administrative authorities lacked the competence and the experts to co-ordinate construction, industry and transport, and to control the movement of manpower accordingly. All these issues came under ministries — either in Moscow or in the capitals of the republics — who were not familiar with local needs or capacities. With the enterprises now able to finance minor modernization or provide housing for their staff, they increasingly demanded responsibility to make more effective use of their means. The way forward — as in foreign trade — was for them to develop contacts directly. The ministries opposed them, but not with complete success, because Party directives now authorized such business contacts. Here, as in other areas, there smoulders a conflict of interests between the Party leadership and the ministries.

Faced with such operational problems, the Party leadership in 1979–83 decreed further measures in support of reform. Short-term planning changes — caused, on the one hand, by continuous ministerial interference in the production process and, on the other, by "disorganization" and "lack of discipline" in the enterprises — were to be combated by stable planning criteria and medium-range plan targets. This aim can be realized only if the plans imposed from above are reduced and enterprises allowed to share in the planning process.

At the same time, social indicators were supposed to become a regular part of enterprise-level and national-level economic planning. The number and qualifications of the workers, the individual wage categories and the mobility of the work-force were all factors to be systematically included in the decision-making process. A few industries and enterprises developed the beginnings of "social planning" and, subsequently, "complex economic and social planning" during the 1970's. But because of the lack of empirically trained sociologists and of socially sensitive managers, there has been little change in existing planning practice in most industries.

Elimination of the two major shortcomings — frequent planning changes and the exclusion of social factors — is possible only with the co-operation of ministries and state commissions. So far, however, their delaying tactics have obstructed the training and employment of suitably qualified sociologists and economists. Nor has Gosplan made any provision for the co-operation of the work forces.

But all this could gradually change once a new, results-oriented, wages policy imposes new social differentials within enterprises. Naturally this presupposes that bonuses, now distributed to all workers by enterprise managements, will be negotiated by trade unions championing the work-force.

On January 1 1984 an experiment was started, initially within the orbit of five industrial ministries, by which enterprise managers were given more authority and scope in planning, production, and allocation of wages and profits. In return they were expected to display greater readiness to take risks — to develop new technologies and new products, enter into delivery contracts, and implement them.

On November 15 1984 the Politburo announced the extension of the experiment to 21 Union and republican ministries. The haste with which the Party leadership, still under Chernenko, demonstrated its eagerness to improve the economic mechanism seemed almost precipitate. The reason was that structural tensions were beginning to develop within management level. In early 1985, Pyotr Bunich, Director of the Research Institute for Communal Economy, assessed the industrial experiments in these words: "Although the individual enterprises are functioning smoothly, the superordinate bodies, such as ministries and industrial complexes, are continuing to operate in the old style." In other words, the experiment has not decentralized the process of investment. Thus the enterprises cannot even theoretically create modern, lucrative concerns.

It thus becomes increasingly obvious — as the Novosibirsk Research Paper (among others) says — that the present system of

management is lagging considerably behind production. Management in the middle level of control — that of the ministries and
administrative authorities — is too complex. By contrast, the top
and bottom levels (the central administrative bodies and the
producers) were progressively dropping out of the organizational
structure. This is where the Novosibirsk Research Paper sees the
real cause of the "administrative fragmentation of economic management, the imbalance in the development of the economy." The
indispensable "transition from predominantly administrative to
predominantly economic methods of management" required a
new system of apportioning influence between social groups, and
this could "not be achieved without conflicts."

Gorbachev would seem to share the basic view of the Novosibirsk Research Paper. As early as April 1983 he stated: "Every
new step in the development of the economy inevitably causes
profound transformations in social, class and national relationships, in the entire political superstructure."

3. ECONOMIC SYSTEM

In the economic system, reforms can embrace the ownership
system, the management structure, the division of labour, and
income distribution. These four elements are closely linked; it is
virtually impossible to change one without the others. Any profound restructuring therefore requires more prolonged prepara-
tion. There is also a need for change in living and working habits.
What is needed, therefore, is co-operation by all groups in society,
not simply decisions by the state and Party leadership. The more
outdated a country's economic structure is, the more deeply
rooted is resistance to reform.

The need for change in an economic system that was set up half
a century ago has further grown as a result of the pressure
produced by the 1965 reform, however inadequate this may have
been. Gorbachev's clear aims will further increase that pressure.
That is the most important result his policy can have in the short
term. In the medium term it would be up to Soviet social scientists to prepare a model of reform, as the Novosibirsk Research
Paper stated. Even though the paper was a synthesis of critical
investigations by Soviet lawyers, economists and sociologists, it
nevertheless complained that the social sciences had not yet
found a fundamental direction for reform.

The social sciences, however, are not about to be included in a
practical sense in research into economic reform. True, *Principal
Directions* assigns to the sciences the task of "intensifying research the results of which would permit far-reaching qualitative

changes in the productive forces." Equipment of research institutions must therefore be "substantially improved." But equipping research organizations has not yet been given much attention. The task of the social sciences consists mainly in "analysing more thoroughly the problems of perfecting developed socialism." "More detailed research is to be conducted into the development processes of the political system, of socialist democracy, the state and socialist self-management...." These areas are of vital significance to the theory and future practice of socialism. The need for improvements in economic management — described in the draft of the Party programme as the indispensable prerequisite of intensive development — is not apparently seen as sufficient justification for a commitment to empirical research.

Traditionally, economic growth depended on the development of new industries, new labour forces, and new regions. And although considerable shortages have since arisen, this does not mean that the whole of the economy is as yet under pressure to modernize. In the Irkutsk economic region, economic growth between 1970 and 1982 was one-third due to extensive growth and two-thirds to increased productivity. In the region's northern area, the share of extensive economic growth amounted to 85 percent. In many regions it is still necessary to develop infrastructure and industry first. For these regions and for these tasks, the old methods of economic management have not entirely lost their validity. Therefore, the authorities can with some justification continue to refer to the old methods, and thus disguise the fact that their power, indeed their very existence, is assured only so long as a transition to intensive economic growth is retarded. There is, moreover, a tendency in the Soviet Union's central and older industrial regions to set up new enterprises in disregard of the latest state of technology and to establish new work places without the manpower being available, instead of modernizing old plant.

Here the centuries-old pattern of reform seems to be repeated: enlargement instead of modernization. When Peter the Great and Catherine sought to reform a backward Russia, they too tried to overcome the inertia of their subjects and institutions by extending their territory and their administrative units, creating something new without abolishing the old. Such tricks are, and always were, expensive; but then the cost of maintaining old economic and political structures counts for little in the calculations of rulers.

The connection between investment practice and productivity in the present-day Soviet economy was recently highlighted by the journal of the State Planning Committee (*Planovoye Khozy-*

aystvo 2/1985). In the fields of planning and financing, the journal said, the industrial ministries continue to give priority to the establishment of new industrial enterprises as against the modernization of old plant. A mere 2–3 percent of machinery and production equipment are renewed annually, although in the view of Soviet economic experts the optimal figure would be 6–8 percent. As a result, industrial plant is largely obsolete. In order to keep it operational, a large number of specialists and engineers are engaged on repairs — technicians who are badly needed in modern enterprises or who might be doing more productive work elsewhere. Industrial repair costs exceed the sums spent on replacements. Moreover, the preservation of old and outdated plant means that far too many operations are still being performed manually in the Soviet Union, making the manpower shortage even worse.

According to the directives of the *Principal Directions,* "investments are to be employed chiefly for the reconstruction and technological re-equipment of existing enterprises; the proportion of industrial construction used for this purpose is to be increased to 50 percent" — as against an average of 30 percent in the past. In the Russian Republic, production is to be stepped up solely by means of technological re-equipment and reconstruction of existing enterprises, and by the application of modern technology.

The introduction of new machines and new technologies demands change in the division of labour. Whereas modern technologies in processing industries are economically viable only for large-scale production — i.e. they presuppose a high degree of specialization — Soviet enterprises have always been characterized by their heterogeneity. Certain products are manufactured in a multiplicity of enterprises, at high cost. It is true that central and regional Party bodies have for years been calling for greater specialization and concentration of production. But the tendency towards self-sufficiency has proved stronger — and not only because of the inadequacy and unreliability of transportation.

In the Soviet economic system, it is the ministries and administrative authorities that lay down production targets; it is they that provide investment finance. The 170 production associations and the lesser industrial enterprises of the Leningrad area, for example, are managed by no fewer that 150 ministries and authorities. Each of these control bodies tackles the problems of technological progress within the framework of its own responsibilities, when in fact an overall solution is called for.

This truth is no longer locked away in the ivory towers of Soviet scholarship. On March 29 1985 it was stated in a fundamental theoretical article in *Pravda.* Because the system of separate industries predominates in economic management, *Pravda* said, the tasks of introducing a unified technological policy cannot be solved. Technical progress, after all, does not necessarily accord with the responsibilities of individual ministries. "The tendency of separate industries to formulate economic interests and priorities," according to *Pravda*, has in fact grown stronger, "which at times runs counter to the interests of the economy as a whole."

"Privatization" has advanced to a point where it even embraces the superstructure. Ministries and state committees have begun to publish their own "political economy," books in which they develop their own special theories. *Pravda* sees this as a threat to the success of the continuing experiment in the 21 industries. It states that an integrated economy should be *"a system for planning and optimizing* production, distribution (and redistribution), and for exchanging goods and demand at a level above that of individual industries."

In order to protect the overall economic interest, the *Principal Directions* stipulates that "the functions and the structure of ministries and other state bodies must be precisely laid down... Control bodies are to be set up for groups of interlinked branches." In October 1985 the Politburo ordered the establishment of a Bureau of the USSR Council of Ministers in charge of machine building. This body would co-ordinate all the various engineering ministries.

On the other hand the *Principal Directions* provides for an extension of the role of research and production associations and of production enterprises. "Any administrative interference, petty guardianship or unjustified reglementation of the economic activity of associations or enterprises, collective or state farms is inadmissible."

The State Planning Commission is to have a totally new task within the system of economic control. At the Central Committee's Technology Conference in June 1985, Gorbachev, invoking Lenin, demanded that Gosplan transform itself into "the country's central scientific economic body." Gosplan's responsibility for the main economic regions and local production complexes is especially emphasized in *Principal Directions*. Discussion on problems of the planning reform since the late 1960's has clearly shown that social and economic development can be more effectively harmonized only at a regional level. How quickly or to what extent these conclusions can be translated into practice is of course a different question.

The imbalance in material and political power between local administrative and Party bodies on the one hand and the central authorities on the other increases social differences and tensions.

Regional state and Party bodies cannot withstand the self-interested demands of the central economic authorities. True, the local bodies were supposed to plan the development of towns, regions and republics, to co-ordinate the individual plans of the separate branches of the economy, and to ensure supplies of goods and services for the public. So far, however, they have been unable to prise from the central ministries and authorities guidelines on measures foreseen and investments available. In such conditions, businesslike relations between central and local bodies are impossible. Decisions from the top can be influenced only by personal contacts or subjective predilections. There is no such thing as a rational choice between projects.

As a result, in many towns enterprises have put up prestige buildings — like houses of culture and sports facilities — that are little used, while supply facilities, housing and clinics are lacking. *Izvestiya* has called the present state of affairs in small towns "hopeless." The cost is huge, in both economic and human terms. A series of articles entitled "Small Town, What's Your Life Like?" began shortly before the publication of *Principal Directions*. The intention of these merciless descriptions of wretchedness were to arouse understanding for the importance of "harmonious regional development" and "the development of small and medium-sized towns."

Simultaneously, however, the idea persists in the public mind that social and economic progress can be made without conflict. The roots of this belief are in personal experiences of Stalin's ideology of violent class-struggle. The longing for domestic peace was (and is) entirely understandable after decades of psychological and physical terror. Yet the belief in utterly harmonious development is a shackle, especially in planning. Each enterprise unit simply writes in a percentage increase in its old economic activity. No change occurs in the producers' scales of values or attitudes. Readiness to accept responsibility or innovation is not encouraged. The creation of incentives — the opportunity to earn more through better work — fails to produce any change. Economic efficiency has not become a social norm.

Russian workers would still rather accept the tariffs fixed by the authorities than wage differentials that depend on their own performance. This applies particularly to results the value of which is determined by the market-place. It is true that many Muscovites will pay high prices for agricultural produce in the markets — a fact which invariably fascinates foreign visitors and makes them believe in the "remedies of the market-place," remedies that are still largely forbidden. What they do not see is the powerful traditions and clear-cut divisions between small retailers and large-scale commercial operations. Both suppliers and customers in the "private markets" belong to minorities: they come from a narrow stratum of the population and from few, mostly non-Russian, regions. The colourful markets in large cities, as well as the existence of the black market, are not evidence of an imminent change in the economic system, any more than state-owned enterprises can unhinge the market economy in the West.

That the roots of free market relations and of commercial thinking do not go very deep in Soviet society was shown by a number of *Pravda* articles in the autumn of 1984. Following outraged readers' letters — whether genuine or fictitious is irrelevant — complaining about excessive prices being charged in collective farm markets, *Pravda* said that to reward higher productivity with higher earnings was not against socialist principles.

Renewed discussion in the press on the earnings of itinerant "brigades" are likewise concerned with the question of a "fair wage." In the work-place, high income is more readily conceded to those in high positions than to those who are merely particularly hard-working. But everyone gets his share. Judging by letters to the editor and by accounts in the Soviet press, it seems to be the practice to pay bonuses even to workers who are often absent through drunkenness or who do unsatisfactory work. In its struggle against "levelling," the new leadership certainly does not have the silent majority behind it. This, too, reveals how difficult and how daring it is of Gorbachev to attempt reform of the country's narrow traditional system.

Soviet citizens preserve their liking for conformity even when buying Western goods. They will pay a month's wages for a pair of jeans. But they will not tolerate any attire deviating from the mass. Western clothes — conspicuous expressions of a progressive attitude — arouse the active displeasure of Russian patriots. And anything that disregards, either in colour or in cut, the monotony of prevailing taste is conspicuous. Some Moscow women artists avoid public transport because their individualistic attire would be likely to attract insults.

The parallels between the private and political spheres are as typical of the Soviet economic system as its contradictions. The attempt to stimulate demand by inculcating new standards of quality and aesthetics was part of a strategy to combat the traditional lack of entrepreneurial spirit in industry.

The Soviet leadership, in its present attempt to awaken a sense of innovation in its enterprises, will find no natural allies either among producers or among consumers. Queues outside Moscow shops are no proof of a demand for reform. Though the buyers are waiting to acquire everyday consumer goods or even prestige articles, their demands are often determined by old habit. New requirements scarcely exist, especially outside the big cities. *Izvestiya* of April 10 1985 reported from the Turkmen Republic that in spite of high incomes the rural population all too rarely exhibited the wish to furnish their homes in a contemporary manner or to acquire a desk for their children. It was therefore important to influence taste and demand among the rural population, for instance through exhibitions and other events. Manufacturers and stores, the paper said, should not only analyse public demand, but create it.

In an industrialized society, such methods are commonplace; but not so, or not yet, in the Soviet Union. My friends in Leningrad were astonished to hear that in the West (and even in their socialist neighbour Hungary) it was customary in shops to find a great choice of articles and courteous assistants. They obviously did not really believe it. So how can they demand something they cannot even imagine? Where no demands are raised it is difficult to construct reforms.

Can these limited domestic impulses be intensified by constructive suggestions and arguments from outside?

Many observers, those who do not view the Soviet system as poised between market economy or ruin, ask whether Hungary could provide a model for the Soviet Union. Even Soviet scientists, Party officials and journalists have begun to examine the successes and problems of their small socialist neighbour. At the beginning of June 1985, for instance, a three-day conference of prominent Soviet and Hungarian economists was held in Moscow to discuss the economic reforms in their countries: the problems of central versus localized control, new principles of pricing etc. The traditions and conditions of the two countries are of course so different that a direct transplant of Hungary's reforms is out of the question. Hungary depends on foreign trade and has to adjust to the world market. The Soviet Union continues to be largely self-sufficient. Nevertheless, it intends to concede a greater role in future to supply-and-demand economics. *Kommunist*, the Party's theoretical journal, maintained this view shortly after Gorbachev's accession, supporting material incentives and the principle of cost-effectiveness.

As for the other features of the Hungarian reform, the Soviet press presented these in piecemeal form. *Pravda* in its issue of April 1 1985 carried an article by Istvan Szabo, chairman of the

15,000-hectare "Red Star" co-operative. Szabo had become a
Politburo Member of the Hungarian Socialist Workers Party only
a few days before. He was thus in a position, with full Party
authority, to explain to the Soviet readers the measures which
had contributed to the success of Hungarian agriculture:

— in the 1960's, the co-operatives were granted a large measure of independence. They thereupon began to organize
their production on a contractual basis and to sell their
produce freely.

— in the 1970's, a close network of inter-enterprise co-operation came into existence; this was not impeded by the state,
in spite of the need for large subsidies. Industrial and service
enterprises took part in this co-operation.

— Szabo played down the contribution made by private farms
and market-gardens to the improvement in supplies and
efficiency. It was not really "private" — as Western journalists were claiming — but closely interwoven with the overall
economy through co-operative arrangements.

The negative side of this development, needless to say, was not
mentioned. It might have made this model even less ideologically
acceptable. As an inescapable result of its new agricultural policy, Hungary has sustained an enormous rise in the cost of foodstuffs, a decline in food quality and increased damage to the
environment.

Another important innovation in the Hungarian economic system has been receiving only selective publicity in the Soviet
press. In *Pravda* of March 23 1985 a Soviet journalist, who had
taken part in a tour of Hungary, reported that major Hungarian
enterprises would forthwith be managed by their own boards of
management. But there was no mention whatever that these
boards were being elected by the workforce and that they were
taking over all the responsibility of the industrial ministries, and
hence also the rights of ownership and use of the means of production.

But these are only individual instances. The "far-reaching restructuring of the economy and the whole system" called for by
Gorbachev presupposes the creation of more general conditions
for reform. The lessons of Hungary show that these are a matter
not so much of ideological decisions as of long-term processes. The
political scientist Mihaly Bihari (*Tarsadalomkutatas* No 2/1985)
has deduced the following seven prerequisites for reform:

— a coherent reform concept;
— commitment to reform by central authorities;
— an adequate power base for continuing reform;
— room for political manoeuvre at home and abroad;

— preparations to deal with opposition democratically;
— creation of inducements to continue reforms;
— formalization of the result to make them irreversible.

Many of these conditions exist in some measure in the Soviet Union. The gradual extension of the rights of work-forces and local bodies in social planning is a consequence of Kosygin's reforms. Its continuation is undoubtedly one of Gorbachev's priorities. Eight months after his accession, he submitted to the Supreme Soviet a Long-Term Plan which envisages a multitude of small steps in that direction.

To sum up: the Soviet Union is under pressure to reform. The principal prerequisite for the Soviet Union is lasting peace and reduced expenditure on arms. There are areas in which change is possible. But as yet a reform model does not exist.

It seems that Gorbachev was able greatly to extend his power base during his first year in office. He and his colleagues now argue for the new course in personal appearances in the provinces. The draft of the new Party programme is discussed in the press and at public meetings with a view to achieving a reasoned consensus.

It remains to be seen whether this approval will overcome the barriers to reform. One such barrier is the attitude, common to both the public and the bureaucrats, that conflict should be avoided, while authority and stability are respected in themselves. The ability to think innovatively is not common — that, at least, was what the *Literaturnaya Gazeta* concluded in self-critical reflections on the Party's draft programme.

The experiences of the other socialist countries — Hungary and Bulgaria in a positive sense, Poland and Romania in a negative one — show that agriculture must be the starting point. Gorbachev the agricultural economist brings to this task both competence and the will for such reform. But he has not so far been able to apply either of these successfully enough for the brigades favoured by him to be granted freedom over their work facilities or procedures. The bureaucracy's fear of losing planning supervision and control still obstructs that indispensable step.

Much the same diagnosis applies to industry. There too the established ministries have so far been almost insuperable barriers. "Central planning authorities and ministries ... are not prepared to delegate additional tasks to enterprises on the necessary scale," *Pravda* complained on April 10 1985 in an article on the newly extended industrial experiment. Under the headline "On the Search for Correct Solutions," it stated: "Without a reorganization of relations among all participants in the production process as well as in the distribution and consumption of the products... the inadequacies will perpetuate themselves."

The reorganization "at the state level" began with a reduction of the ministries. In order to cut down radically on the number and the power of the industrial ministries, Gorbachev needs allies in the economic system itself. These he can find among the managers of large-scale industrial and agricultural enterprises as well as among economic experts. A mere four weeks after his election, the new Party chief invited representatives of these groups for a talk with top officials of the Party. At that meeting, according to *Pravda* of April 9, "a frank discussion" took place of many topical problems.

In the long run, a reorganization of economic relations is possible only by way of a legal reform. True, the lawyer Gorbachev possesses the specialist knowledge to implement it. But whether he can find the necessary political consensus and the organizational drive remains to be seen. What is, however, certain is that the next few years will witness increasingly fierce conflicts.

Mikhail Gorbachev is at least making the attempt to turn bureaucratic paternalism into a limited pluralism of interests — and that is something new in Soviet history.

Mária Huber is a Research Fellow at the University of Heidelberg. She is a specialist in the economics of Eastern Europe and the Soviet Union.

APPENDIX 2

The Men Behind Gorbachev

In his selection of Gorbachev appointees, Christian Schmidt-Häuer outlines the careers and characters of 18 men who are representative of the new generation of leaders.

YEGOR KUZMICH LIGACHEV

Ligachev is the chief Party ideologist and — after Mikhail Gorbachev — the most successful Soviet politician of recent years. It was only in April 1983 that Andropov brought him from Siberia to be leader of the Central Committee Department for the Organization of Party Work and thereby entrusted him with the register of Party members.

Thus equipped, Ligachev became the most effective administrator that the Soviet Union had had for a long time — at least in the area of personnel policy. He mercilessly demoted and pensioned-off corrupt and incompetent bureaucrats and inferior Brezhnev proteges. Tirelessly, he conducted the selection of candidates for regional Party committees, for the election of the Supreme Soviet, and for the composition of the new Central Committee. After Gorbachev's accession, Ligachev became No. 2 in the Party — a full Member of the Politburo; Central Committee Secretary for Ideology, Cadre Matters, and External Affairs; Chairman of the Foreign Affairs Commission of the Supreme Soviet of the USSR.

Superficially, there could hardly be a greater difference between Gorbachev and Ligachev. Gorbachev tends to extemporise freely, stresses form, is restrained but extroverted and often speaks with an intimate style, while Ligachev rattles off his texts in a loud voice and with a monotonous rhythm. There is nothing inspiring in the way he talks. But despite appearances he is quite unlike the grey Old Guard of Brezhnev and Chernenko's day. He is a man who is obviously impatient with delay and seems full of energy. Like Gorbachev, but in his own style, he makes very clear his commitment to force on Soviet bureaucracy the criteria of an achievement oriented society.

Yegor Ligachev was born on November 19 1920. He trained as an engineer and during the war his work in Novosibirsk exempted him from service at the front. He joined the Party in 1944, at 24, and started his political career as Secretary of a local Committee of the Komsomol in Novosibirsk. According to A. Asarkan, a Soviet journalist now living in the West who is the main source of information on Ligachev's early career, Ligachev's rise through the Komsomol was apparently rapid, and by the end of the 1940's Ligachev was already forceful and supremely self-confident. According to Asarkan, he was removed from the office of First Secretary of the Komsomol because of *vozhdism*, a presumptuous style of leadership. But he cannot have been considered incompetent, for he was enrolled in a correspondence course at Moscow's higher Party school. At the same time (1949—51) he worked as the lecturer of the Novosibirsk City Committee of the Party, and rose to departmental head of first the City and then the District Party Committee.

In 1957, he had his great chance, thanks to Khrushchev. In May of that year, when the Siberian department of the Academy of Sciences was established and the science-city of Akademgorodok was hacked out of the taiga, Ligachev, at 37, was given the post of First Secretary of the local Party. He was responsible for construction, travelled more frequently to Moscow, met planners and ministers, and got to know the top Soviet researchers, among them a number of reform-minded scientists in favour of the Siberian project.

With his next move, Ligachev began his career as a campaigner against corruption and indiscipline. At the beginning of 1959, the First Secretary of the District Party Committee and the Chairman of the District Executive Committee were accused of defrauding the state in the course of grain purchases, and fined. Ligachev was lucky: a former colleague from the Moscow Institute for aviation construction, Fyodor Loshchenkov, moved up to the post of Second Secretary of the District Committee, and appointed his old friend as Party secretary for ideological matters.

The pair were so successful that in 1961 Khrushchev had the two of them brought to Moscow. Ligachev started off as Deputy Head of the Central Committee Department for Agitation and Propaganda. A writer and a critic of the regime, with whom I discussed those years in Moscow, remembered that the new man from Novosibirsk adopted a pronounced anti-Stalinist posture. In 1963, by now 43, Ligachev was made Deputy Head in the Central Committee Department for Party Organization, the department to which Andropov reassigned him 20 years later.

In November 1965, a good year after Khrushchev's fall, when Brezhnev had to make room in Moscow Central for his own proteges, Ligachev was made Party secretary of the West Siberian oil and natural gas region of Tomsk. He remained in this post for almost 18 years. And although he was made a Candidate Member of the Central Committee in 1966 and a full Member in 1976, time appeared to pass him by. In fact he used these years well.

He quickly made a name for himself as a man who, while insisting on discipline and efficiency, was not vain, narrowminded and orthodox. In 1968, he became Chairman of a commission for youth matters, newly set up by the Supreme Soviet. It was then that he had his first close contact with Gorbachev, who, in 1974, succeeded Ligachev as Chairman of the same commission. In Tomsk, where he remained until 1983, Ligachev tried particularly to achieve better labour discipline through better organization. He cut by almost half the meetings of Party, trade union and other social organizations and campaigned successfully against drunkenness by creating a "narcological service" to cure alcoholics.

In character, he remains as astringently puritan as ever. In June 1985, Radio Yerevan in Armenia gave Moscow Television's news programme an unusually long one-man show. Before an enormous bust of Lenin, the bull-like Ligachev, thick strands of grey hair sticking up above old-fashioned horn-rimmed glasses, hammered away at the comrades of the Armenian capital. In a throaty voice, pushing out his words in hard, regular bursts, he read the riot act to those in the hall. It was as if a rough, solid master-craftsman was explaining the strict regulations of his middle-class enterprise to some southern villagers. "More energy!... Personal responsibility!... Decisive strengthening of discipline!" the stocky speaker thundered down from the lectern. "Spongers will no longer be tolerated!" The only joke which he permitted himself was involuntary, the result of overzealousness. He told Armenia, the Soviet republic with the best brandy and the fewest alcoholics, that it was not enough for its inhabitants to modify their drinking habits — there was to be no more drinking at all!

Ligachev's career is rooted in the conviction that modernization involves not simply discipline but also improved social policies. Not that this is a simple matter. Ligachev's speeches and published statements as chief ideologist reflect the problems.

In June 1985 Ligachev told the Academy of Social Sciences: "The changes which we have developed in our discussions will take place within the sphere of scientific socialism, without deviation to a market economy or private enterprise." Many observers saw in this a renouncement of all experiments which had been expected in the West. In reality, Ligachev's statement to the Academy — a sort of ideological holy shrine — was nothing more than a propagandist truism. There was far more to be read into Ligachev's statement that the experiments for expanded independence and greater accountability by industrial concerns were to be carried out "without departing from the social programme, from full employment and from the interest in improving material standards." It is this that shows how carefully the new leadership needs to proceed — looking over their shoulders at social unrest in Poland and the social inequalities resulting from the Hungarian and Yugoslav reforms, with the resistance of their own bureaucracy and the fundamental supply problems staring them in the face.

Ligachev's own statements often reflect the difficulty of preserving balance. Before the Academy of Social Sciences, he pleaded strongly for more control. On the other hand, in a key article in *Kommunist* in August 1985, he complained about the results of such control: hundreds of thousands of workers were losing too many hours in discussions, seminars and volunteer work.

Similar conflicts exist between the work ethic and better use of leisure. In *Kommunist*, Ligachev condemned the practice of many citizens who neglect their work because they are too heavily engaged in sporting contests and amateur activities. On the other hand, the provisions to combat alcohol abuse — of particular concern to Ligachev — foresee the creation of new leisure centres and sports facilities, and thereby up-grade commitment to recreation. Such conflicts, and their resolution, are part of political reality. And Ligachev, though no reformer, is a realist, dedicated, as Gorbachev is, not to the victory of world revolution, but rather to the nuts and bolts of constructing a better form of socialism in their country, and thus creating out of the Soviet Union an economic superpower, and not just a military one.

NIKOLAI IVANOVICH RYZHKOV

The new Prime Minister of the Soviet Union is a good advertisement for the nation that Gorbachev wants to fashion. He looks like an alert, youthful senior civil servant from a capitalist country. He cuts a splendid figure, but he keeps a low profile. Like Foreign Minister Shevardnadze, Ryzhkov initially stood in Gorbachev's shadow.

The second youngest Member of the Politburo (after Gorbachev), Ryzhkov is not a career politician. He has spent almost his whole career in industry — as foreman in a smelting works, as head welder and as works manager in the weapon forges of the Urals — and he was never active in the Party apparatus. It was not until 1981 that he became a member of the Central Committee.

Ryzhkov, born on September 28 1929, was moulded by the Urals and by Sverdlovsk. He was briefly a mine-worker, and then in 1950 started as a shift leader in the S. Ordzhonikidze heavy machine construction works in the Urals. As he rose, he studied engineering at the Polytechnic Institute, which he left in 1959.

In the first half of the 1970's, Ryzhkov was director of the Uralmash production association, the gigantic conglomerate that is central to Soviet defence industry. He thus came from the entourage of the man who was long seen as the "crown prince," Andrei Kirilenko, Party leader of the Sverdlovsk region from 1955 to 1962. Even then, he was already an extremely important man for Moscow, as was shown when in 1974 he also became Secretary of the Commission for Planning and Budgetary Matters in the Union Council of the Supreme Soviet.

A year later he moved completely to Moscow and took on the office of First Deputy Minister for Heavy and Transport Machine Construction. In 1979 he became the First Deputy Chairman of the State Planning Commission (Gosplan). There he gained the experiences which were to aid Gorbachev in binding the Planning Commission closer to the Party to provide overall economic guidance.

In November 1982, immediately after Brezhnev's death, Andropov took over Kirilenko's personal retinue, among them Ryzhkov, who had been a Central Committee member for only a year. It was Andropov who plucked Ryzhkov from obscurity, and made him Central Committee Secretary, responsible for building up a new department of co-ordination, thus beginning the attempt to limit the planning bureaucracy and achieve better management of the industrial processes.

After Andropov's death, Ryzhkov left no doubt about where his loyalty belonged. In his speech for the elections to the Supreme Soviet in early March 1984, he brusquely ignored Kremlin ritual by mentioning Chernenko's accession to power only in an aside.

Ryzhkov has generally given away little about his opinions, least of all on defence matters, which is surprising for a man from the heart of heavy industry. He confines himself to the usual demands for "appropriate defence forces to hold up any aggression." Nor has he defined his proposals for the expansion of consumer goods industries, public services and structural changes in any great detail. As Prime Minister, he has the advantage over his predecessors in office in that he knows the problems and processes in the production associations and major industrial concerns down to the last nut and bolt. But he remains something of a light-weight. As Central Committee Secretary he was additionally responsible for Comecon before his appointment as Prime Minister, but he hardly travelled abroad beyond his Eastern European area of responsibility. It seems likely that this head of government will remain a loyal and uncontentious assistant in the shadow of the Secretary General.

VIKTOR MIKHAILOVICH CHEBRIKOV

Chebrikov, Director of the KGB, made his mark publicly in a remarkable speech a few days before the Geneva summit, on November 6 1985, at the traditional ceremony on the eve of the anniversary of the Revolution. He was unprepossessing, and his speech was dry and unemotional. Yet no one could ever remember having heard such a speech on such an occasion.

For Chebrikov summed up Gorbachev's demands as no one else had done, coolly and without any empty rhetoric. It was astonishing that the head of the KGB of all people should speak of "reforms" — a word that was used extremely rarely in Gorbachev's first year in office. People usually spoke of "reconstruction," "refurbishments," "revolutionary transformation," "period of transition," or "changes."

Chebrikov offered 5,000 representatives of the Soviet elite some further unusual expressions: "extension of personal rights and freedoms," "room for direct criticism of shortcomings in principle," "turning-point," "acceleration of socio-economic development" and "transparency" — a particularly ironic word for a KGB boss to use. He did without any of the usual threats against dissidents and warnings of "ideological subversion" from the West. As regards the Military, he restricted himself to the standard formula: "We are under the obligation to maintain the defence capability of the Soviet state up to the necessary standard." Speaking of the forthcoming summit in Geneva, he said in a statesmanlike and conciliatory manner: "We are of the opinion that much can still be rectified, if one is prepared to show political courage and a capacity for rapprochement."

The message was unmistakable. Firstly, in the name of the Kremlin leadership, Chebrikov was sending out a signal of moderation before the summit. Secondly, the fact that the State Security chief was chosen to speak on this occasion underlined the principle that the KGB was among the strongest supporters of Gorbachev's "reconstruction."

Chebrikov seems an unlikely contender for high office. With his fixed expression and large horn-rimmed spectacles, he cuts a morose figure. Moreover, he came from the very place whose "clan" had come under fire from Andropov and Gorbachev at the beginning of the 1980's — Dnepropetrovsk.

Born in the Russian Republic on April 26 1923, he attended the city's Metallurgical Institute after his war service, and left it in 1950 as a qualified engineer. There are a number of famous names among its old boys, including Nikolai Tikhonov and Leonid Brezhnev. Chebrikov remained in the Dnepropetrovsk "family" for a long time. In 1951 he left his profession to join the Party machine; in 1961 he became First Secretary in the Dnepropetrovsk Party organisation; and from 1965 to 1967 he was Second Secretary of the District Party Committee.

Chebrikov did not become a KGB officer until 1967, when Brezhnev brought him in as head of Personnel Administration in the KGB. Only a year later, he was promoted to become a deputy chairman of the KGB, a post he held for the next 14 years.

Then suddenly, from the end of 1981, events began to move very quickly. With the help of his allies in the KGB and in the Party leadership, Andropov started his campaign against the corruption of the Brezhnev clan. After Brezhnev's brother-in-law and First Deputy Chairman of the KGB, Semyon Tsvigun, failed in his attempt to protect Brezhnev's relatives and died (probably by his own hand), Chebrikov was appointed as Tsvigun's replacement. A few weeks later, in May 1982, Andropov became Central Committee Secretary, ridding himself of the office of KGB Chairman, which he had held for 15 years but which he now saw as an obstacle to his progress. His replacement, Vitali Fedorchuk, whom Brezhnev had sent to the Ukraine in 1970, was a stop-gap. All the indications are that in the conflict over Brezhnev's succession, Chebrikov came down firmly on the side of Andropov and Gorbachev and thereby against the Dnepropetrovsk clan. Immediately after Brezhnev's death, in December 1982, the new

General Secretary Andropov appointed Chebrikov as KGB Chairman.

Under Gorbachev, Chebrikov's role is to reflect Gorbachev's policies, aimed as they are at more discipline but also at more openness and an improved international image. The fact that he used a mild and appealing tone in his November 1985 speech was in keeping with Moscow's tactical line before the Geneva summit. But even on other occasions, when Chebrikov has spoken about the KGB's tasks, his arguments have sounded quite different from what might be expected. Shortly after Gorbachev came to power, Chebrikov published an article (*Kommunist*, No. 9/85) under the heading "Follow the example of Lenin and the demands of the Party." While previous published contributions from the KGB overflowed with melodramatic tales of secret agents and enemy activity, conspiracy theories, and attacks on Western intelligence organizations, Chebrikov was considerably more relaxed and less hysterical. He confined himself to vague propagandist commonplaces like "ideological subversion," "bourgeois propaganda," and "anti-Soviet centres." He only attacked the United States once, and elsewhere he even pointed out the value of democratic principles in international law. All in all, Chebrikov displayed restraint and moderation towards the West.

Partly, this reflects Gorbachev's decision to strip the KGB of its grim anonymity. Today passers-by can leave carnations at a memorial for Andropov at the ochre walls of the Lubyanka building headquarters of the KGB — always in the past a place of terror, particularly under Stalin. In the summer of 1985, Gorbachev sanctioned a sentimental film that presented Andropov as a great humanist, showing his Lubyanka office with reverential intimacy.

Does this mean that the lot of dissidents — whether moderate critics, human rights activists or outright opponents of the Soviet system — will become easier under Chebrikov and Gorbachev? Certainly, they want to avoid acts of revenge that damage the Kremlin's image without increasing security. This may mean tolerating more criticism — but not decreasing surveillance. Active dissidents will continue to feel the power of the KGB. The careful experiments and structural changes in the economy must after all be secured.

VITALI IVANOVICH VOROTNIKOV

To general surprise, at Chernenko's lying-in-state on March 11 1985, there stood at Gorbachev's right hand a man who by rights did not belong there, according to the precisely defined hierarchical order of Politburo Members. Indeed it was the first time Vitali Ivanovich Vorotnikov, 59, had appeared so obviously at Gorbachev's side.

Vorotnikov has been more of an industrial administrator than a purely Party organizer. He was born on January 20 1926 in Voronezh, in the Don area. In 1942–44 he completed an apprenticeship as a locksmith in the railway engine repair works in Voronezh. He joined the Party in 1947 and completed his studies in 1954 at the Aircraft Institute in Kuibyshev.

Like Ryzhkov, Vorotnikov comes from Andrei Kirilenko's entourage, and during the latter's ascendancy he became First Deputy Prime Minister of the Russian Republic. In 1979, after his mentor's fall, Vorotnikov in 1979 was packed off as Ambassador to Cuba. In 1982, Andropov, gathering up Kirilenko's dispersed entourage to form his anti-corruption brigade, recalled Vorotnikov. It was on Andropov's orders that Vorotnikov cleaned up the south Russian province of Krasnodar, which had previously been administered by Brezhnev's corrupt friend, Sergei Medunov.

But since then Vorotnikov has not always pulled his weight as a reformer. In June 1983, he became Premier of the Russian Republic and in December 1983 a full Member of the Politburo. As such, he made obeisances to the new General Secretary Chernenko that clearly went beyond the restricted politeness which the Gorbachev group was showing in its dealings with Brezhnev's heirs. In his speech for the elections to the Supreme Soviet in February 1984, immediately after Andropov's death, Vorotnikov praised the memory of the 25th and 26th Party Congresses — milestones of Brezhnev's rule. The remainder of Gorbachev's team referred only to the Central Committee meetings since Andropov's accession, as if this represented the beginning of a new era.

Judging by his speeches, since his return from Cuba and his ascent into the centre of power, Vorotnikov, of all Andropov's heirs, is the one who has pressed least for improvements in consumer goods production and for "transparency." At most, he supported the "completion of the existing economic mechanism."

On the other hand, as Prime Minister of the Russian Republic, he helped to undermine Moscow chief Viktor Grishin and his entrenched clique; and he has not curbed open discussion. *Sovietskaya Rossiya*, the newspaper of the Russian Republic's government, and once a boring and strictly Russian-nationalist broadsheet has become the most interesting daily newspaper in the Soviet Union (it exposed the Moscow construction fraud and has printed occasional articles by Khrushchev's son-in-law, Alexei Adzhubei).

EDUARD AMBROSIEVICH SHEVARDNADZE

Shevardnadze, the Soviet Foreign Minister, is an unusual man. He was born on January 25 1928 in the small west Georgian village of Mamati. His father was a teacher. One of his brothers, Ippokrat, who died in 1978, was an influential departmental head for trade, planning and finance in the Georgian Central Committee, and promoted the career of his younger brother. Eduard Shevardnadze studied history at the Kutaisi Institute of Education and at the Georgian Party Academy. At the age of 20 he joined the Party, and for a decade he was engaged as an activist in the Komsomol. In 1961, he changed over to the Party apparatus. Three years later he joined the Ministry for the Maintenance of Public Order (that is, the Ministry of the Interior), initially as First Deputy Minister then, in 1965, as Minister.

In this post he got to know the whole extent of corruption — the fencing of stolen property, the black marketeering, the nepotism, all ineradicable Georgian traditions, but at that time operating at an unprecedented level under the then Party leader, Vassili Mshavadnadze. In 1972, the corruption consumed its children. Mshavadnadze went and Shevardnadze arrived. The new Party leader was given the task of draining the Georgian swamp and setting the economy back on a sound footing.

In Moscow tales soon spread of good St. Eduard's battle with the evil Georgian dragon. Many of the glowing reports that emanated from Tbilisi have since been confirmed to me by Georgian intellectuals. The new Party leader moved through the land berating the people with Old Testament rage: "We Georgians, a people of farmers, heroes and poets have become thieves, cheats and black marketeers!" When at a meeting of Party members, hands were raised to vote, Shevardnadze saw on countless wrists a glittering array of Swiss and Japanese watches and threatened to confiscate the lot unless he got his way. Apocryphal or not, these tales helped to create the image of a Mr. Clean which made Shevardnadze a natural member of the Gorbachev inner group. When he departed for Moscow in July 1985, he had not been able to defeat corruption totally, but the economy had improved considerably.

Roughly at the same time as Gorbachev began agricultural experiments in the Stavropol Region, Shevardnadze did the same in Georgia. In 1973, in the west Georgian town of Abasha, he grouped all agricultural institutions into one management association. At the same time, those who worked on the land received material and financial preference, following the Hungarian example. The "Abasha experiment" led to a rapid increase in agricultural production. (Later, it was expanded, with varying degrees of success.)

In his time as Georgian Party chief, Shevardnadze made his mark securely, in a remarkable path towards democratization within the framework of the Soviet system. Admittedly, many proud Georgians still accuse him of being a closet Russian — they can never forget that at the 25th Party Congress of the Georgian Party in 1976 he declared in the flowery language of his people: "For us Georgians, the sun does not rise in the east, but in the north, in Russia," and he always eulogized Brezhnev. But behind these fine words he promoted both economic and sociological experiments and a renaissance of Georgian cultural tradition. Georgian films became a cult among international film buffs, who enthused about the works of Otar Yosselyani and Dhengis Abuladze. For many Western European cities, Tbilisi became a mecca of cultural exchange.

Shevardnadze also managed to control traditional Georgian antagonism, not only towards Russian hegemony but also towards the national minorities within their own borders. Georgian Jews were permitted to emigrate almost unhindered. It was to test the mood of his own nation that Shevardnadze set up the Institute for Opinion Research, the institute that analysed corruption in Georgia.

Shevardnadze's personal courage is legendary. In 1977, during a football match between the local team, Dynamo Tbilisi, and a team from the Russian Republic, anti-Russian demonstrations broke out among the Georgians following a disputed penalty. Shevardnadze himself went on to the playing field with a megaphone and persuaded the brawling fans and truncheon-wielding police to withdraw amicably: "The referee's decision will be checked tomorrow!" he yelled. "Now go home!" Admittedly, the referee was prevented from leaving the Georgian capital the next day by irate fans blockading the airport, but in the end anger died away more rapidly than if the police had had the last word.

In 1978 thousands of students demonstrated against the draft of a new Georgian constitution, according to which Russian was to join Georgian as an official language. Only about one fifth of all Georgians speak fluent Russian. The demonstrators collected in front of the Party building and the situation looked like turning ugly. Once again, Shevardnadze addressed the crowd: "What are you doing, my children?" he shouted, angrily. They answered in chorus: "We are not your children!" Shevardnadze, however, refused to be cowed. He heard the demands, negotiated, went to Moscow and insisted that Russian should not become an official language in Georgia.

He has shown himself willing to admit his own shortcomings. In 1983, he confessed to *Pravda* that for too long he had doubted the reports of corruption concerning the Georgian Minister of Finance, Parnaoz Aniashvili. In July 1983, at the Plenum of the Central Committee of the Georgian Communist Party, Shevardnadze declared: "When I call upon comrades to point out shortcomings in the functioning of the Central Committee, then of course I have in mind the work of the First Secretary as well. Like any other human being I have my faults, and I would like members of the Central Committee to point them out. All the more so since these faults are not the result of a lack of desire on my part to work better. It is simply that I cannot always manage to do everything. Sometimes I do not have the time, sometimes I lack the necessary ability or experience."

Gorbachev, who had meanwhile risen to become Central Committee Secretary for Agriculture in the Kremlin, showed a particular interest in Shevardnadze's work in agriculture. The two already knew one another from their Komsomol days two decades earlier. Now Gorbachev made several journeys to see his old friend and to gather information, in December 1980, January 1983, and — most notably — in January 1984 while Andropov was on his deathbed, when they would certainly have discussed the question of the succession.

On July 2 1985, the Supreme Soviet appointed Shevardnadze Foreign Minister as Gromyko's successor. Though watching diplomats were incredulous, Gorbachev had acted with great skill. He had not acquired an expert, but instead a man of wide talents — imaginative, capable, charming and one who would not prevent Gorbachev from making his own foreign policy and thus gaining in status as a statesman. In addition, Gorbachev had drawn into the innermost circle of power the most original and reformist regional politician in the Soviet Union, one who is known both as a disciplinarian and a man of action.

Shevardnadze seems to reflect Gorbachev's own opinions and character. Centralism may be the "point of departure in economic organisation," Gorbachev has said, quoting Lenin, but "our principal task consists in creating a maximum of initiative and allowing as much independence as possible out there in the country." No other Member of the Politburo has in recent years acted as much in the spirit of Lenin's words as Shevardnadze.

GEYDAR ALIEVICH ALIYEV

Next to Chebrikov and Shevardnadze, Aliyev is the third man in the Politburo (he has been a Member since November 1982) who has a past as a security official. An Azerbaijani born in 1923, he served 20 years in the KGB, and was KGB Chairman in the Republic of Azerbaijan from 1967 to 1969 before becoming Party chief.

The Party gave him the same task as Shevardnadze in 1972: to stop corruption in his home region. Aliyev became the scourge of the Azerbaijani bazaar bourgeoisie. Unlike his neighbour Shevardnadze, he did not develop a commitment to the modernization of social structures, but his efforts led to considerably increased economic growth rates in Azerbaijan.

An imaginative and astute organizer, he was given by Andropov the almost insuperable task of improving the transport system, one of the most important prerequisites for a more rational economy. His success, or lack of it, remains unclear. In any event, in Gorbachev's first year in office Aliyev was far less in the foreground than expected by many Western observers, who at times had even seen in him a serious contender for the post of Prime Minister.

ABEL AGANBEGYAN

This academic economist from Armenia is the respected leader of the Novosibirsk Economic Institute, from which in 1983 emanated Tatiana Zaslavskaya's criticism of the centrally planned economy, the so-called Novosibirsk Study. Aganbegyan does not belong to the circle of leadership, but he is one of Gorbachev's most important advisers.

He moved to Moscow to become Chairman of the Commission for the Study of Productive Powers at the Presidium of the Academy of Sciences of the USSR. Aganbegyan looks less to the Hungarian reforms than to the modernization of the economy of East Germany. He pleads for large-scale interwoven industrial associations that are to be furnished with independent financial resources for production and research. His public pronouncements during Gorbachev's first year in office were no more informative about the proposed structural changes than Gorbachev's speeches. But indirectly they sounded a note of warning — that the measures which had been instituted so far were insufficient to decentralize responsibility and create sufficient incentives for workers on the shop floor.

NIKOLAI VLADIMIROVICH TALYZIN

Talyzin was born on January 28 1929 in Moscow. From the age of 13, he worked as an electrician. In 1955 he graduated from the

Institute for Telecommunications in Moscow. Later he completed a doctorate in technical sciences and achieved the title of professor. For a quarter of a century, he has been with the Ministry for Telecommunications, taking over as Director in 1975.

His responsibilities also reached into sporting and even military fields. He belonged to the organizational committee for the 1980 Olympic Games. And when Soviet troops marched into Afghanistan at the end of 1979 he was reported to have been staying in Kabul. In 1980 he rose to become Deputy Prime Minister and represented the Soviet Union in Comecon. The few press conferences that he gave revealed him as skilful and informative.

In October 1985, he moved to centre stage, becoming Chairman of the State Planning Commission (Gosplan) and thereby successor to the orthodox, 74-year-old Nikolai Baibakov, who had held this office since October 1965. On the following day, Talyzin also became a Candidate Member of the Politburo and one of the three First Deputy Prime Ministers.

This man, with his widespread knowledge of technical and state administration, is one of those technocrats with whose skills Gorbachev wants to modernize the Soviet system. In Gorbachev's words, Talyzin is supposed to help "to realize Lenin's idea and to transform the Planning Commission into a scientific-economic organ" no longer dictating quantities for industry, but rather developing yardsticks for quality.

VIKTOR PETROVICH NIKONOV

Born in 1929 as the son of a peasant, Nikonov took on, in April 1985, the thankless task of Central Committee Secretary for Agriculture, the post which had been Gorbachev's springboard to power. Unlike Gorbachev, however, Nikonov had never bothered much about anything other than agriculture. Graduating as an agronomist, he headed in turn an agricultural college, a machine-tractor centre and the Central Committee Department for Agriculture in the Krasnoyarsk region, before becoming the Minister for Agriculture of the Russian Republic and finally Deputy Minister for Agriculture of the Soviet Union. In all these capacities he has had links with Gorbachev for years.

BORIS NIKOLAIEVICH YELTSIN

Like Ryzhkov and Vorotnikov, Yeltsin, who became Central Committee Secretary for Construction in July 1985 and six months later took over from Viktor Grishin as Moscow's Party chief, comes from Kirilenko's former personal entourage, which

Andropov took over. Born in 1931, Yeltsin attended the same Polytechnic in Sverdlovsk as Prime Minister Ryzhkov. He specialized as a construction expert and rose within the Party to become First Secretary of the Sverdlovsk Region. He held this office from 1976 until April 1985, when Ryzhkov brought him to Moscow as a Central Committee Departmental Head.

LEV NIKOLAIEVICH ZAIKOV

Central Committee Secretary for Defence Industry since July 1985, he succeeded the deposed Grigori Romanov (as he had previously succeeded him as First Party Secretary in Leningrad). Romanov had passed this office on to him in 1983 when he moved to Moscow, even though Zaikov had previously only held leading positions as a director general and in the government machine, never a proper Party post. It is not known how he performed during Romanov's gradual ousting from power. During his grand tour of Leningrad in May 1985, Gorbachev addressed Zaikov in a demonstratively intimate manner with his forename and patronymic — significant public gestures at a time when Zaikov's erstwhile patron Romanov was being eased out of the Politburo.

ALEXANDER N. YAKOVLEV

During the Geneva summit in 1985 there was one member of the Soviet delegation whose name meant very little to many observers. But this small stocky man, with his large, bald head and his brown protruding eyes, is almost always present on Gorbachev's travels. Whether in Canada, Britain, Siberia or Kazakhstan, Yakovlev was always part of the group.

Gorbachev's versatile advisor, who since summer 1985 has been Head of the Central Committee Department for Propaganda, is one of the brightest figures in Gorbachev's entourage. Forward-looking, open-minded, tough, obstinate, aggressive, he does not mince his words.

Born in the Russian Republic in 1923, he served in the Army from 1941 to 1943, graduated from the educational institute in Yaroslavl and worked for seven years for the Party apparatus in the Yaroslavl Region. From there he went to Moscow, was initially Deputy Head of the Central Committee Department for Science and Culture and from 1956 to 1960 attended the Party Academy of Social Sciences. At the end of the 1950's, he lived for several months in America as a Soviet exchange student at New York's Columbia University. In the 1960's and the 1970's, Yakov-

lev wrote a string of books about American foreign policy. He
completed his studies of historical sciences with a doctorate and
from the early 1960's, successfully pursued his career in the
Central Committee Department for Propaganda.

He was acting head of the Propaganda Department when it
drifted into a long-running conflict with the Cultural Department of the Central Committee over the nationalist line adopted
by the Komsomol journal *Molodaya Gvardiya*. Yakovlev — just as
temperamental, aggressive and polemical then as he is today —
wrote a 10,000-word attack on the Russite nationalists under the
heading "Against Anti-Historicism," demanding that authors
should cease to idealize the "stagnating daily life" of the Russian
village. They should, he said, show greater interest in the internationalism of Marxist-Leninist ideology. Shortly after his article
appeared, the troublesome Yakovlev was sent off to be ambassador to Canada.

There, he prepared Gorbachev's May 1983 visit. A month later,
Gorbachev brought him back to Moscow.

It was with Yakovlev's advice that Gorbachev acted against the
Russites after his visit to the Moscow Artists' Theatre in spring
1985.

What effect will Yakovlev's recommendations in foreign policy
have? While Gromyko's sights were largely on America, Yakovlev planned for growing "polycentrism" in the West. In an interview with the Italian newspaper *La Repubblica* (May 21 1985), he
described international politics as "multi-polar." Besides the United States, he looked towards Western Europe and Japan as
centres of power. China, Brazil, Canada and Australia, he said,
would all increase in importance.

Gorbachev put forward similar ideas in a statement of principles on ideological matters in December 1984, when he was still
No. 2 in the Party. Significantly, he did not adhere to the usual
view of the Americans as the swaggering leaders and seducers of
the capitalist world. Rather, he saw "a gradual but ever clearer
loss of America's earlier economic and political hegemony".

It was noticeable that in the run-up to the Geneva summit, it
was Yakovlev who continued to mount the sharpest attacks
against the United States. Thus in a discussion in *Literaturnaya
Gazeta* (June 26 1985) he stated: "In their calculations and plans,
the Americans do not rule out the direct unleashing of a war
against the Soviet Union, if the political and military leadership
in the US views the balance of power as favourable to such a
solution."

VADIM ZAGLADIN

Clever and persuasive, Zagladin, of the Central Committee Department for International Relations, is an expert in ideology and political theory, and has been known for years in the West as a sort of travelling salesman for the Party. His views make him a moderate. As early as May 1979, Zagladin (with I. Frolov) declared in *Pravda*: "In the world as it is today, even a partial solution of global problems requires the co-operation of states belonging to opposite systems." And further: "Concrete researches that are widespread in the West regarding special (principally scientific-technical and technological) aspects of global problems contain a number of interesting, positive elements.... Marxists should not underestimate that."

FYODOR BURLATSKY

Burlatsky is a member of the circle of advisors and publicists who stood behind Andropov. In 1983, when Andropov, already a sick man, was trying to reduce the influence of the Military, Burlatsky published in *Literaturnaya Gazeta* an unusual account of the Cuban missile crisis in 1962. Its message was that politicians must keep a tight rein on the Military.

As a framework for this warning, the author used a discussion between Kennedy and his crisis management staff improvised from American and Soviet documents. The core of these discussions is a dialogue between the Kennedy brothers on the risks that develop when the Military participates in a political decision. The Army, says John F. Kennedy, should not even be allowed to make military decisions, because the Military are the first to lose their head in a crisis. Robert agrees. The Military are conservatives, he says, who act according to the order of battle of past wars. It is true they have the best knowledge of nuclear weapons, but they ignore the necessary military and political conclusions. Robert concludes that if the Cuban missile crisis had not been solved through the superpowers' secret diplomacy, the Military would have toppled the President and seized power.

The message in Burlatsky's fable has since been reflected in Gorbachev's moves to rein in the Military and to initiate dialogue with America.

GEORGI RASUMOVSKY

Born in 1936, Rasumovsky took over from Ligachev the Department for cadres in the Central Committee, or to give it its correct title, the Department for Organizational Party Work. Before the 27th Party Congress, this department oversaw the composition of the new Central Committee. Ironically, Rasumovsky did not even belong to the Central Committee when at the beginning of June 1985 he became the personnel director to the Party (in which capacity Ligachev continued to look over his shoulder).

Rasumovsky trained as an agronomist and started his political career in 1959 in the Komsomol and in the Party in the south Russian region of Krasnodar, Sergei Medunov's notorious den of corruption. At the end of the 1960's, Rasumovsky, then just 30, was running the region's agricultural department. Since Krasnodar borders Stavropol, it can be assumed that even then Gorbachev knew of him. Later the two of them co-operated directly. When Gorbachev had risen to be Central Committee Secretary for Agriculture in Moscow, Rasumovsky temporarily headed the Department for the Agro-Industrial Complex in the Council of Ministers of the Soviet Union.

In June 1983 Rasumovsky was promoted to become First Secretary of the Krasnodar Region — in other words he became successor to Vitali Vorotnikov, who in 1982 had been sent by Andropov to clean up the mess left by Medunov. Rasumovsky continued the clean-up. In 1983 and 1984, as he wrote in *Kommunist* in March 1985, half the Party Committees in both city and region were changed — a sufficient recommendation for his new job.

ALEXANDER AKSYONOV

The appointment of this man to be the new Chairman of the State Committee for Television and Radio in mid-December 1985 is also indicative of Gorbachev's style. Aksyonov, 61, previously ambassador in Poland, is also an ex-security official. In 1959–60 he was Deputy KGB chief of Byelorussia, and then the republic's Minister of the Interior. Later, he took on numerous senior Party posts, before becoming Byelorussian Prime Minister in 1978. As ambassador in neighbouring Poland, following General Jaruzelski's assumption of power, he sought the progressive "normalization" which Gorbachev espoused in Warsaw shortly after he took office. Aksyonov's role is in effect to mobilize the media to make Gorbachev's appearances more effective and to improve the flow of critical information — but at the same time to keep a tight rein on these processes.

VSEVOLOD MURAKHOVSKY

In 1978, the 52-year-old Ukrainian became Gorbachev's successor as First Secretary of the Stavropol Region. He was formerly Gorbachev's superior in the Komsomol and had furthered Gorbachev's career in the Komsomol and the Party. Later, as Party chief in Kislovodsk, his contacts were useful for Gorbachev. On November 1 1985, the Secretary General brought him to Moscow to become one of the three First Deputy Prime Ministers and take over the newly-created state Committee for Agro-Industry (Gosagroprom), which now directs parts of the agriculture and the food industry.

YEVGENI VELIKHOV

A 50-year-old nuclear physicist, combining a peasant look with sophisticated worldly experience, Velikhov is Gorbachev's scientific adviser. Experienced in Western ways, knowledgeable about the Soviet Union's technical and scientific difficulties, he sees the future in terms of exchanges with the rest of the world, not in isolation. According to American experts, Velikhov has provided a decisive contribution to the development of the Soviet laser programme. This alert, energetic physicist appears to be the most likely candidate to succeed Anatoli Alexandrov, the octogenarian President of the Soviet Academy of Sciences, an organization whose importance will be increasingly felt as modernization proceeds.

INDEX

Index compiled by Frank Dunn